"In the introduction to her book, *Almost a Princess*, Jane Rubin writes, "At this point, I am feeling a bit possessive about my life and need to tell my story in my own words." And yet, in telling her own story in a voice so intimately first person, her "possessiveness" results in a generous sharing of her life, her battles, her fear, her vulnerability, her perseverance, and her ever deepened humanity as she faces life's imperfections. Divorce, the loss of her younger brother, not one but two cancer diagnoses, and so much more could have left her broken, cynical, hopeless and afraid of loving in the face of inevitable loss. But she is anything but. This book is overflowing with her joy of simply being alive, her boundless love and her hard-earned wisdom that no moment, great or small, can be taken for granted.

With humor, with grace and with wisdom, she takes us along on her journey of self discovery and it becomes our own. Reading of her hope gives us hope. Learning of her healing helps us with our own and gives us insight into the inner world of the patient as person. Reflected in Jane's words, I saw my own experiences of love and loss clarified and illuminated. And for this, I am ever so grateful."

Rabbi Donald B. Rossoff
Temple B'nai Or
Morristown, NJ

To Amy
Any friend of
Dale's is a
friend of
mine
Jane

Almost a
Princess

My Life as a Two-Time Cancer Survivor

JANE LOEB RUBIN

iUniverse, Inc.
Bloomington

Almost a Princess
My Life as a Two-Time Cancer Survivor

Copyright © 2011 Jane Loeb Rubin

iUniverse books may be ordered through booksellers or by contacting:

iUniverse
1663 Liberty Drive
Bloomington, IN 47403
www.iuniverse.com
1-800-Authors (1-800-288-4677)

ISBN: 978-1-4620-0240-5 (pbk)
ISBN: 978-1-4620-0241-2 (cloth)
ISBN: 978-1-4620-0242-9 (ebk)

Library of Congress Control Number: 2011904124

Printed in the United States of America

iUniverse rev. date: 4/7/2011

To those who have struggled with serious health challenges
and are determined to live each day to the fullest.

Contents

Just a Pair of Patent Leather Shoes 1

Bombs Away! 4

Don't Look Down 11

Wear the Jewelry 15

Complete with Headlights 17

A Rattle Would Have Worked Just Fine 19

The Sewing Tsunami 22

An Early Lesson in Loving Life 24

All I Want for Christmas Is My New Front Teeth 27

I Thought His Name Was Sven, But It Probably Was Shlomo 29

My Sister Ann 32

Here Comes the Sun 36

I Never Lived in My Childhood Home Again 39

You Know It's Over When … 43

Single and Scared 45

Teenagers and Transitions 52

A View from the Other Side of the Drape 54

The Cancer Etiquette Dance 60

Reflections: One of My Favorite Role Models 64

How I Met My Husband 70

When I Need a Quick Chuckle 74

It's Time to Begin Chemotherapy, Again 76

The Lows and the Highs 79

The Quail 82

My Name, Just Two Four-Letter Words 85

WWJD 88

All in a Name 91

"Mom, How Does It Really Feel?" 94

Tennis Lessons 96

I Think I May Have Killed My Wig 100

Lessons from a Triathlete 102

To Sleep or Not to Sleep 105

Our New Lake Home 108

Oh, Baby! 111

Who's Been Eating the Nuts Off of the Coffee Cake? My Yom Kippur Confession 113

Free Fall: The Final Frontier 115

Role Reversals 118

Soft Breathing 121

Newton's Third Law 124

The Third Act 127

Acknowledgments

This effort would not have been possible without the endless stories, support, and encouragement from my beautiful family, professional colleagues, and dear friends.

A special thanks to Nancy Gross, who introduced me to the art of narrative medicine and its healing qualities two weeks before my most recent diagnosis, and to Lisa Goldberg Ozer, who spent hours poring carefully through every page with red pen in hand. Her feedback was immeasurably helpful.

My deep gratitude to an outstanding medical team at Atlantic Health in New Jersey: the physicians, nurses, technologists, and hospital well-wishers who continually kept a supportive, open mind to my needs as a patient and individual.

And, of course, a very special thanks to David, my husband, in-house editor, and sounding board, who helped me find my voice.

Introduction

I am a two-time cancer survivor. After a diagnosis of breast cancer at the age of forty-six, I thought about documenting my experience in writing but never followed through with it. I don't know whether it was a sense of immortality, or maybe denial, but I took my medicine, so to speak, and moved on. I had just gotten engaged after twelve years as a single parent and was in no mood for a cancer downer.

The first time around, I found the lump in my breast while soaping up in the shower, only two months after my mammogram. It was no one's fault. I was relatively young, with dense breast tissue, and mammography was in its earlier stages. Fortunately, the cancer was also young and had not yet reached my lymph nodes. But through blood work during my treatment, I discovered that I had a genetic mutation, often found in Eastern European Jews, leaving me highly vulnerable to more breast cancers and ovarian cancer as well. My family's cancer history sent up red flags, too. Two of my first cousins had ovarian cancer. One is an eleven-year survivor and sadly, the other one, Laura, passed away a few years after she was diagnosed. But the hardest hit of all was witnessing my younger brother, Leo, succumb to cancer eighteen years ago when he was only thirty-seven years old. Clearly, the likelihood of a genetic defect was high. So, I took the chemotherapy and underwent seven hours of preventive surgery (including the removal of my ovaries) with, I must say, a beautiful reconstruction job. I thought I was free of the curse at last.

When I got the breast cancer diagnosis, I was engaged to my soul mate, my companion slipper, a man I never would have had the antennae to find when I was younger but so very lucky to have discovered in this chapter of life. He has been a rock and a wise, positive, loving friend through our marriage and cancer journey. He has truly accepted me for who I am. We married after I finished my chemotherapy treatment and surgery in 2001. At our wedding, our children held the chuppah and the rings. It was, for both of us, one of the most joyous days of our lives.

Over the last ten years, I have done my part to religiously monitor my health, diligently following up with blood work and physicians' visits. Unfortunately, thanks to the thoroughness of my team of experts, a new cancer was recently discovered. Apparently, a sneaky new devil was able to sidestep my long-gone ovaries and set up shop in my peritoneum, the casing that holds in all of the digestive organs. The cells in this abdominal tissue are very similar to the ovaries and respond to the blood tests for ovarian cancer. A series of scans and a biopsy confirmed the diagnosis.

I always knew that there was a small risk of this happening but emotionally chose to function as if there were no risks. So it took a couple of weeks for me to get over the shock. After all, I had been filleted and what seemed like eviscerated ten years back, just to avoid such a calamity. I had allowed myself to feel like cancer was a bad dream in my past. This time, though, it feels very different. I have many reasons to be optimistic, but at the end of the day, I am a realist, and my stories should help explain why. I know that even if I beat this cancer, there may be others waiting for me in the next decade, or my body may not respond to the poisons quite so effectively this time around. Only time will tell.

So I have chosen to write and document some insights about myself in a set of essays, including my life, my philosophy, and my experience as a cancer survivor. I am also at an age when I often find myself at funerals for relatives and parents of friends. Our parents' essence, abbreviated histories, and long lives are filtered through the words of rabbis, clergy, and family members. At this point, I'm feeling a bit possessive about my life and need to tell my story in my own words.

I set out on a writing journey of self-discovery, looking for my voice and challenging myself to seek a deeper self-understanding as I faced this fearful disease. In the end, I learned some of the endless ways to heal and stay positive. Essays were the choice *du jour* since I am a memo writer by profession, and my thoughts seem to come in sound bites. I always thought of my life as ordinary, but I have learned through this journey that we are all special with a unique and personal story defining us.

To those who read my book, I hope that you will understand who I am. I know that my grandchildren will read these stories someday; through them they will meet their Grandma Jane and get a glimpse of the different time I grew up in. And for my special comrades, those of you facing cancer or a life-altering disease, I hope some of my reflections resonate in a way that brings you hope, strength, and peace.

I chose the title, tongue in cheek, because I do believe I have had close to a perfect life and have no right to complain. I grew up with parents who loved me and have siblings and friends I treasure. As my father often said, "I never missed a meal," and "I had the world in the palm of my hand." The first time around, I married a man, David, with whom I shared some of life's greatest adventures: parenthood, exploring the globe, and living happily as a young couple, even though we were poor as church mice. I have incredible children who bring bottomless love and endless miracles to my life every day. I have become a grandmother this year. Words cannot describe the deep love I feel for my granddaughter. I have had a wonderful career in healthcare and believe that my efforts have made meaningful contributions, raising the level of care in my community. My second husband, also David, and his children have been the icing on the cake. Our blended family did not form later in life by accident. I believe we were all meant to be together.

The title *Almost a Princess* is really about the cancer, the disease that steals away the feeling of perfection. *Almost* is the key word because we all know there is no flawless plan and life is just a short visit on Earth. Like everyone else, I have experienced disappointments from time to time in my circumstances, in others, and even in myself, but those frustrations pale in comparison to this horrible disease.

I have learned that survival and quality of life come down to embracing what we are given each day, doing the very best we can with it, and feeling the joy and fulfillment that comes with our past, present, and ongoing life stories.

Just a Pair of Patent Leather Shoes

Didn't we all fantasize about being stars when we grew up? Even a little bit? I sure did.

In the 1950s that meant to me, and many other girls of that era, ballerinas, princesses, Shirley Temple, and perfect little Barbie dolls (which, by the way, had just come on the market). What we wanted to be when we grew up usually didn't include doctor, lawyer, or rocket scientist. For those of us heading into the professional world, it more typically was teacher or nurse. Our futures were heavily defined by the external tangibles rather than self-actualization: husbands, children, homes, and cars. That didn't come for women until the late 1960s.

Growing up as just about the only Jewish girl in a community saturated with christening gowns, frilly confirmation dresses, and "Sunday best" attire, I was, by definition, different. My parents had their own way of doing things when it came to just about every aspect of our family life, and religion was no exception. I knew there were lots of Jewish children in the town next door, but our family did not belong to the synagogue, so I rarely met them. I had no understanding of what being Jewish was all about. As a result, I struggled to sort things out in a lonely quest for self-definition. My parents had no hint of my need to feel a sense of belonging outside the walls of our home. From my standpoint, they seemed happy with things just the way they were. They certainly had no clue, nor any inclination to learn the choreography needed to get inside my little head. But I didn't understand any of that stuff at five years old. All I wanted was a new pair of shoes.

Little children are extraordinary creatures. In my little girl head, with my simple logic, I made myself believe that I would fit in perfectly

1

if I could only convince Pop, my very practical, Depression-era father, to buy me a pair of black patent leather shoes like the neighborhood girls wore on Sunday. They were the trophy, the tangible symbol of my deepest motivation to define myself as a special little princess. Dorothy had her ruby slippers, and I was certain that if I could hold those shiny black shoes in my hands and slide them onto my slightly oversized feet, I would be lifted to the highest heights of princessdom and my sense of self-worth would soar.

Pop said my all-purpose leather shoes were perfectly fine for all occasions other than gym class, and he wouldn't budge. He held firm, refusing after countless rounds of five-year-old reasoning, bottomless puddles of tears, tantrums, and breast-beating to grant me this wish. Over several years, my sister Ann, family friends, relatives, my mother, and even Pop's friend Herb, the owner of the local shoe store, tried persuading him to give in, but not my father. He never really understood or cared about my need to feel like an insider. It took until later in life for me to understand that those shoes symbolized something entirely different for him, an important lesson that would take many years for me to fully appreciate.

Fast-forward to a visit home from college in the early 1970s. Pop and I were relaxing in the living room and reflecting on my childhood years. He was boasting that he had knocked the ball out of the park raising me; that he had molded a strong and capable young lady who was ahead of her time, because I had lived a perfect childhood, just like a princess! Wow, did that ever strike a sensitive cord. Finally, after all those years, I had an opening to get the old grudge out and set the record straight. I reminded him about the shoes, and the trauma his practicality had inflicted on my childhood. Pop let out a gigantic laugh, one of his trademarks, and after sharing his amusement that I even remembered such ancient history, he explained to me for the first time what had been on his mind back then. He strongly believed that learning to accept life's disappointments built character, and that my own ability to do so would build strength, channel my energy in productive directions, help me stare down adversity, and teach me to forge ahead with the force and drive I would need to obtain important things in life. If I still wanted the patent leather shoes along the way, well … I could buy the damn shoes myself. He still thought they were a waste of money, and he saw absolutely no value in trying to be like anyone else.

I had to hand it to him. I was pretty adept at taking my hard knocks, brushing myself off, and getting back on track. I poured my energy into college, projects, and all sorts of interests that I collected along the way. Even now, instead of feeling sorry for myself, most days I use my energy in positive ways.

But back to the shoes. I still believe that Pop probably could have found a better way to make his point with a small child, and with a lot less drama. But somehow, when I look at the few cute pairs of patent leather shoes I chose to buy and cram into my overstuffed closet, I can't help but be reminded of one of the many important lessons Pop taught his five-year-old daughter. As far as defining self-worth by external tangibles, well, suffice it to say, I am still working on that one.

Bombs Away!

It is hard to understand me without knowing my father. His persona was so large that it overshadowed all of us at home. For the most part, that was okay, since Pop had a funny, generous spirit, but at times it crowded out the family stage. Although Mom often served as a buffer, she happily played second fiddle to my father in a quest to love and keep him happy. Mom was like the mortar holding a stone wall in place. Most folks notice the stones, but without the mortar, they fall down.

Robert Victor Loeb, otherwise known to his children as Pop, was a street-smart Brooklyn guy. Born in 1923, the middle of three sons, he developed a quick sense of humor and unmatched loyalty to his family and friends. He lived by the rule of measuring others from their actions and deeds, not words. When Pop died, my husband described him to the rabbi as "large and in charge." That said it all. But to those close to him, we could also see that beneath the public façade, a fire burned deep within him.

Pop was a World War II veteran who served in the Pacific as a navigator/bombardier flying a B-25. He was typical of many veterans of that war, filtering his stories to his wife and children but mostly choosing not to discuss any details. He preferred to simply wear the pride of having served his country.

What he did choose to share were the maverick stories, the ones that made his platoon sound like characters from an Indiana Jones movie or *Hogan's Heroes*. Army life for his young platoon was at times what frat living was for my son: full of testosterone-driven antics. For instance, there was the time they took a pet monkey on a flight mission. As playful young men, they had befriended a wild macaque on Okinawa. After one mission with their new pet on board, Pop's flight crew had a few drinks and convinced themselves that this animal brought good luck. A few weeks later during another mission, the wild monkey defecated on the aerial map smack in the middle of their flight path. So, my twenty-one-year-old navigator father replotted their course around the small brown pile rather than cleaning it up. What other choice did they have? When the team arrived back at the base hours late with only a few drops of fuel remaining, he and his mission team were threatened with a court martial. Pop's superior officer had been rightly afraid that the men were gone for good and couldn't get over their adolescent thinking. As far as the threat of a court martial, what could possibly be the grounds? Without precedent, flying around monkey poop would set an embarrassing first and very likely also implicate the commanding officer. Plus, they all knew that it wasn't the first time they had flown with the monkey. Thinking about it later, my father concluded that his superior officer, a man close to the ripe old age of thirty, probably needed every trained soldier he had, especially the daring ones. So in the end, they were ordered to just ditch the monkey, and all was forgotten.

There was also the time Pop's plane was shot down and he and the others ended up on their life raft equipped with scotch and a few other staples. We never heard who set up the emergency provisions on that life raft, but I have a sneaking suspicion that my father had a hand in it. As the story went, the raft was adrift for two days, all the while surrounded by a school of sharks. The men agreed that if their fate was to be eaten by sharks, they were going to get good and drunk first. After drinking for the better part of those two days and the predictable sickness that followed, Pop swore off scotch for the rest of his life. He would never talk about who lived and who died on that mission. I was sure there were plenty of memories that he tried to forget.

Pop kept most of his sobering war stories deep inside until his later years. Retired and bonding more with his remaining friends at their weekly Tuesday lunch group that convened at the Enter Diner, named after the sign they often drove past while looking for the entrance, these stories slowly began to emerge. Bombing villages of innocent people from the sky did not lessen the responsibility he felt, or the daily fear he lived with as a young soldier. Not exactly frat living. During his tour of duty, he also served as the flight medic, administering transfusions, morphine, tourniquets, and bandages to men pierced by the bullets that passed easily through the thin skin of their planes. More than occasionally, these young soldiers died in his also young arms. But, like most men of his generation, he kept those sensitivities under lockdown and only shared them with war buddies, men who understood the half sentences and respectful pauses. The rest of us in his daily life were left interpreting the sudden change in his mood or disproportionate temper following our normal childhood antics with great puzzlement and intimidation.

His emotionally charged upbringing may have led him and his brothers to enlist in the war and fueled his drive to become an officer. His parents, Julian and Helen, were from German Jewish families that came to the States in the 1800s, years before Ellis Island. They were both extremely bright and well educated for their generation, viewing themselves as a cut above the eastern European Jewish immigrants who arrived years later. I am not sure what drove this arrogance, but it may have been their ability to speak English and the extra generation of education and savings they had. Interestingly, Helen's parents had a working farm in Harlem before high-rise buildings there were even a dream. I never found out how Pop's parents met, but they both came from aristocratic Jewish families, or so we were told. Helen swore that she and her sister Abby were Rothschild descendants, but they were never able to make claims to the family fortune because critical records were destroyed in London during the WWII air raids.

Unfortunately, whatever wealth Julian and Helen did have vanished years earlier in the Great Depression. During those awful years, their fighting eroded the family. Helen and Julian's three sons became street tough and learned to fend for themselves, sometimes even stealing food from cart vendors when there were no meals to be had at home. Thankfully, there were relatives of sorts, cousins Miriam and Ralph, who owned a delicatessen and kept the boys full with pastrami sandwiches and pickles, a taste Pop never tired of his whole life. Eventually, his parents' marriage ended, and my grandparents went their separate ways with new partners. The fact that their sons continued looking out for them, including helping Grandpa make his alimony payments from time to time, and later helping them both physically and financially during their last decade of life, always struck me as selfless and generous.

For anyone of my generation, all of this would have landed us on the therapist's couch. But in Pop's case he just toughed it out. After the war, he married Gilda, his childhood sweetheart, a pretty young girl he knew from Brooklyn's Lafayette High School, who devotedly and quietly stood by him through thick and thin. He did his best to earn a good living and create a family of his own. But his early wiring never changed much. In his final years, when hospitalizations became more common, we would find a flask of whiskey in his coat pocket, his added sense of security for potential pain relief and an interesting reflection of his lack of trust in others. My sister, a nurse, commented that this was not unusual behavior among war vets of his generation who more often than not during battles needed to administer their own pain relief.

My father's influence on my upbringing and values was profound. There were periodic clashes at home, particularly during my adolescent years. But in spite of it all, his child-rearing style equipped me to deal with life's unexpected bumps and disappointments. Pop set the stage with his huge presence and peculiar life philosophy. Through it all we enjoyed what was before us and stayed on guard for the worst.

For example, as youngsters we were never allowed to whine. Pop associated that behavior with spoiled, manipulative children, and he had no tolerance for it. We were expected to keep a stiff upper lip and handle the frustration of not having our way from time to time. If we didn't, we were sent to our rooms until we regained control. As we got older, persuasive reasoning would sometimes work, since Pop always liked a good debate. My cousin Don once tried a governmental argument when attempting to reason with Pop. Don scoffed that decisions weren't being made democratically in our house. Pop replied, "Who said this family was a democracy? As far as I'm concerned, it's a kingdom, and guess who's king?!" But as one could imagine, this dictatorial attitude often led to others' frustration and resignation. As a small child, I eventually became adept at holding back the tears. Over time, the desire to cry faded away. It is amazing that I am as demonstrative now as I am, although, thanks to Pop, I can wear a pretty good poker face when the need arises.

Early on, we were taught the difference between wanting and needing. The challenge always came after asking for something material. Since "need" was benchmarked by Pop's austere upbringing, most answers were obvious. We were often reminded how great we had it and how little we deserved to complain. The lifelong impact was both good and bad. To the positive, for many years I was an excellent saver and could easily resist spending temptations. But eventually I began to wonder whether I was withholding treats from myself because I didn't feel deserving. I managed to resolve that conflict a few years back. The proof is in my closet and jewelry box. But I still remain careful with money.

Pop was roped into his second career by some army buddies, after a brief stint as a pharmacist. His friends needed a regional salesman to sell ovens to the bakery industry. Over time, that grew into outfitting entire bakeries with equipment. His high integrity and smart, funny personality led him to become very successful. In the early years, my father would bring my sister and me along on his visits to ethnic customers as props, while he deftly crossed the cultural divide and made the sale. Introducing the common ground of family values worked, and we were rewarded with freshly baked cookies and Pop happily singing show tunes the whole ride home. There were times when our entire family was invited to dinner at his customers' homes. I often remember the dinner at the M's house when my mother's notorious disinterest in cooking was revealed. While facing a table full of savory homemade pastas and meat dishes, I innocently asked Mrs. M what particular cans they came from. I wanted my mother to buy them too. I sat in wonderment when everyone started laughing. Through that experience and many others, I began to see that finding the common ground was a meaningful way to gain trust and develop long business relationships, a very valuable lesson.

My ability to turn my head away from adversity and look for humor and distraction comes from Pop. People tell me that he was one of the funniest people they ever met. His natural ability to flip a fast, clever comeback was a sight to behold. He was once asked by an Egyptian baker if he had ever been to Egypt. Pop explained that his relatives were from Egypt. "As a matter of fact," he said, "they helped build your pyramids." Or the time a German baker was grilling him about the interior capacity of the bread-making oven, to which Pop sarcastically replied, "Don't worry; it seats six." His customers couldn't get over his chutzpah, but he got both of those sales.

Some of his humor was more canned and, for us insiders, a little more practiced as it was replayed for numerous audiences. For example, he often told people that by seventeen I had been asked three times to be married: twice by him and once by my mother. This usually got a good laugh from his audience but sent an interesting challenge to me as a young girl. I was never quite sure how eager he actually was to see me married off. Do you think it was just a coincidence I was married to my first husband at nineteen?

Since so much of Pop's early life was spent outside of the mainstream, it was second nature for him to think creatively when it came to life solutions and adventures. We were told over and over that the world was in the palm of our hands, that there was nothing we couldn't achieve if we put our energy and mind to it. He taught this by example. Buying homes, going to college, and traveling the world were great new adventures for his generation, ones he embraced with enthusiasm. But as his wealth grew, he never forgot those who helped him along the way. For a long time I wondered why we could not pass a Salvation Army collection point without answering the bell with a quarter. Eventually he shared that the Salvation Army helped his family make it through a tough patch during the Depression years and later provided assistance to some war buddies who needed a hand. So now, somehow I feel the same sense of debt and always make a contribution when I see the man in uniform ringing his bell.

Most important, as a child I always felt safe when I was with Pop. He just seemed in constant preparation to slay the dragon if it dared to appear, and that made me feel like I could try anything. Unfortunately, there was no balance of emotion. I never saw Pop's vulnerable side. He did not show his tears to any of us when his brothers passed away or when my younger brother, Leo, died from cancer a few years later. Nontraditional in any religious sense when it came to matters of death, my father and mother kept to themselves after Leo's death, leaving my sister and me to sadly grieve alone. There was no funeral, memorial service, or Shiva.

My last memory of Pop, as he lay on his own deathbed in the ICU, was him telling me to take care of my mother and get her home, as he worried about her night driving, or getting upset by his condition and reminding me where all of the important papers were. I knew then that he had passed the baton to me. He had groomed me for his role, all along with his message, "Take care of your mother and the family." Sadly, in spite of the trust we developed over the years, we were never

9

able to say in words how much we loved each other; something I do so naturally with my own family. But the sentiment was always packaged in our actions. As a result, and as much as I adore hearing those precious three words, I have learned to mainly judge others by their behavior, his final lesson to me.

Gilda and Robert: first date, Western Union delivery, wedding

Don't Look Down

Years back, when I was nervous about facing breast cancer surgery, my husband would say to me, "Don't look down. Think like a tight rope walker and just look ahead to the platform at the end of the rope." It was a very helpful image that kept me focused on a positive goal and gave me a secure feeling. I have used it frequently ever since, usually while waiting for the results of my six-month follow-up testing.

Now, as I face another cancer challenge, I think about that advice and other times in my life when I have felt trapped in a frightening place and needed to get to the other side. One very vivid memory comes to mind.

When I was in second grade, Mom and Pop built a lovely summer cottage on a lake in northwest New Jersey, about an hour north of our year-round home. I think they were able to afford it because, like many Depression-era survivors, they hung onto their pennies not wasting money on the very broadly defined category of unnecessary things, like black patent leather shoes. It was a simple, beautiful paradise, and I loved it. I spent every summer of my childhood there, swimming, canoeing, hiking, and sailing. It was a magical place filled with treasure hunts, homegrown summer stock theater, aquariums, vegetable gardens, and countless games of Ping-Pong and Monopoly. Since no motorboats were allowed on the lake except a state police patrol boat, the air was quiet and peaceful, opening the window for creative play and exploration.

Pop loved to see me take on challenges. At the lake, the biggest challenge was learning to sail solo and participating in the Sunday races between Memorial Day and Labor Day. I was about ten or eleven when I began entering the races. Of course, there were prizes involved, but my goal was to cross the starting line on time, hold my own in my class of boats, and become a force with which to be reckoned.

In order to sail, or head out on the lake alone in any of our boats, we had to prove we could swim across the mile-wide lake one time. Once we made the swim, we were good to go for the rest of our childhood. This feat was a summer ritual performed under the watchful eyes of our parents and next-door neighbors, who had three children the same ages as us. The rule was that we could swim any style we wanted (or no style), but if we touched the rowboat, the challenge was over, and we had to wait until the next year to try again. When my turn came, I remember the overwhelming fatigue I felt about half way across, wishing for the feel of the lake's floor under my feet. Finally, an eternity later, I was surprised by rocks under my feet, so unlike the sandy bottom we had in our swimming area. One by one, year after year, the six of us swam across the lake.

Our folks created this challenge to give us a sense of empowerment. They wanted all of us to realize that the distance to a shore would never be more than half of the swim we faced on those days. Of course, our parents also knew that this logic violated boating rule number one, *never leave your boat*, but they made us do it anyway. Thankfully, I made it across on my first try.

Once sailing on my own, I was fairly capable in my little Sunfish, named *007*, and enjoyed being out in my boat alone, strategizing the fastest way through the course. Racing involves negotiating the wind, avoiding collisions with less-skilled sailors (like myself), and engaging in the polite sailor's version of trash talk. It was a lot of fun, at least until the day the weather suddenly changed and a terrible storm hit the lake. I was dead center in the middle, at least a half mile to a shore. The clouds blew in so fast that I was caught totally off guard. There were no alarms or warnings, certainly no Doppler forecasts; no one saw it coming. At first I thought that it would be just a little drizzle, but within minutes, darkness filled the air and lightning pierced through the sky. The rain was so heavy it formed a waterfall cascading down the sails directly onto me. The wind seemed to be blowing from all directions at once, and I could not harness the sails to direct the boat to shore. I was near panic, stuck, afraid, and alone. How could something this dangerous happen to me? I had never felt so much fear in my life. Mother Nature had unleashed her deadly forces on me for the first time.

My adrenaline level must have been very high, because I remember feeling jumpy and needing to take action. I forced myself to concentrate on my options. I knew the boat was fiberglass, and I was pretty sure that lightning wouldn't strike the body of my Sunfish. I was safe sitting on it. The mast was aluminum, so I did not touch the metal. Swimming was out of the question. In spite of our swimming feats, we had endless reminders of "Never go into the water in a storm!" Being in the water was the fastest way to fry if lightning hit the lake. I had to stay in the boat. Again, there was only one motor boat on the damn lake, but even if it had been nearby, it was impossible to see me through the heavy rain. No one was going to come and save me.

Suddenly, the storm was gone. It vanished as fast as it had come. The club was sounding the horns, calling off the race. I grabbed the ropes and pulled in the sails with my shaking hands, steering the sailboat home. A strange calmness descended on the water. All I could hear were people calling out, "You okay? You okay?"

I could see the panic on my parents' faces a quarter mile from the shore. They were standing on the dock calling out to me. I had never seen them so frantic. It was at that moment that I felt my first taste of being a grownup: capable, like it or not, of holding steady in an emergency and finishing the job. I had always thought that the grownup feeling would come differently, like fitting into a bigger size. I wondered how often grownups felt fear. Until then, I thought the emotion was reserved for children.

I understand so well now that we all have storms we get through in life. Although there are people who care for and love us, there is also a lonely part of the journey we must get through on our own. It is at those times that we must remember the lessons we have been taught and the mantras that reassure us. Together they will help us get through the storm. When it gets scary, it is often best not to look down. Just lock your eyes forward and hang onto the sails.

Summers at Swartswood Lake

Wear the Jewelry

A week before my most recent abdominal surgery, while getting dressed for work, I examined the mundane jewelry I was putting on. As usual on workday mornings when I am trying to get out of the house on time, I was on autopilot, but that day I had to stop and laugh at myself. My surgery was scheduled in a week. Why was I pretending nothing was different?

So, in an effort to feel a small degree of control in my otherwise powerless corner, I opened the home safe to check out my options and noticed some pretty earrings I had bought a couple of years before. I was able to afford these pretty baubles by trading in the "old boyfriend" gold bracelets and necklaces. Some of you might know what I mean by this. They are the shallow trinkets single women collect over the years, like those necklaces with little hearts dangling from chains, dangling like most of those relationships did before their inevitable endings. Along with the trade-in jewelry, I added a chunk of my own hard-earned money that I had been saving and treated myself to a set of expensive diamond studs. They went right into the safe and have rarely been worn since. I sighed, realizing that my practicality was not adding much value to my life. I had to try to change that. So I put on the diamond earrings and immediately felt a little glow.

Around noon, I was washing my hands in the ladies' room at the office and noticed the earring on my right ear drooping down, hanging almost completely out of my earlobe. The back clasp was missing! A wave of panic ran through me, almost as lightning fast as the news of my recent cancer diagnosis. The thought of losing a precious stone evoked the exact same reaction. My immediate next thought was, "Was the follow-up testing like the back clasp? Will it turn out to save me?"

I have been thinking a lot about near misses. We have lots of them in life; most of them never become catastrophes when we are vigilant. Like the back clasps that keep your earrings from getting lost, I will trust that the regular appointments I have adhered to might save my live or at least add time to it. And as far as the diamonds are concerned, if they make me feel good, then I will not hide them away in the safe. I will pull them out, wear them, and sparkle!

Complete with Headlights

Ten years ago, my second husband David teased me about my lack of modesty. By the end of my first encounter with cancer, I had seen so many physicians he was convinced that everyone in the hospital had seen me naked. Like childbirth, when I simply submitted and gave up my privacy to anyone coming through the door, I lost it once again moving through the cancer experience. There was an endless line of doctors and nurses who felt, cut, bandaged, and reexamined my body. It is hard to stay modest when so many people are looking.

After what I then referred to as my "big" operation, I felt so overstuffed with medicine and any professional connected to it, that I just wanted to stay far away. I recovered from a full hysterectomy, bilateral mastectomies, and trans-flap surgery after six months of chemo. It was a rough operation and an even rougher recovery. I had my second wedding to look forward to in four months, and I did not want to go near a hospital any time soon. It was simple: I just wanted to feel well again and have fun. But there was still one thing left to do: nipple reconstruction. This procedure needed to be scheduled separately; after everything else had completely healed. I just wanted to block it out.

After my big operation in 2001, I looked a lot like a rag doll with lines of stitching around my abdomen and breasts. My bellybutton, lost for a while during the surgery, was discovered just in time to secure it back in place. Having been somewhat partial to it, I was relieved later to know that the surgeons did not give up the hunt until they found the lost button. I laugh when I think about them searching for it. The closest I can imagine is when I help friends look and feel for missing contact lenses on the floor. In the OR it must have sounded like, "Oh, where did that damn button go? Is it over by her liver, behind her small intestines, or maybe it rolled over to her diaphragm?"

Weeks later, looking in the mirror, I could not help but marvel at the results. My breasts had not been that perky in years, and the tummy tuck that came with the trans-flap surgery helped give me my old figure back. I was practically in fighting form. Strangely, I kind of liked my new body.

After my honeymoon, complete with plenty of adorable camisoles to disguise the absence of nipples, I revisited the plastic surgeon for a follow-up visit. He convinced me that I could not omit the nipples. Like it or not, he said, "You cannot leave off the headlights." Now he had my attention. Having traveled to Alaska on our honeymoon without worrying a moment about those cold temperature detectors, I had all but forgotten the nipples. Hearing the mandate from a nice-looking man made me wake up and realize the importance of those two small details. So once again, I added another surgery to my calendar and tried in the meantime to stay busy and keep my mind on other things.

Finally, the day came for the procedure. It was an outpatient surgery. After passing through a few nursing checkpoints, I arrived in the surgical staging area. My plastic surgeon, Dr. F, met me there with his entourage of nurses and residents. Once again, I whipped open my gown and let him examine me. He pulled out a red Flare pen and began to draw on my breasts, locating the exact places where he planned to attach the pseudo-nipples. It began to occur to me that the nipple destination was arbitrary. I asked him why he was choosing those specific locations and suggested moving one over a bit. Word of advice, do not ever try to correct a plastic surgeon in the moments before your operation. He gave me a look that could kill.

In awkward situations when all else fails, I typically just laugh at myself, at others, or at the situation at hand. So I laughed, and then finally, he did too. I was assured by Dr. F that he really did know what he was doing, that he was an artist in his profession. A mirror was pulled out for proof, and I discovered that much like nail shaping in a salon, the operator's perspective is usually better than mine. I exhaled and remembered the words on my pre-surgery guided imagery tape: "Your professionals do this every day. Try to relax and let them concentrate on the job. It will be over before you know it." And I did just that.

A Rattle Would Have Worked Just Fine

The week before my recent surgery, I was feeling a need to show my children how much I loved them. One might think that a life of unconditional devotion was enough, but I was still looking for magnanimous ways to show them how much I cared. My first marriage ended early in parenthood, and I have always felt sad and guilty about it. I am a dreamer, and when my first husband (now known around our household as *D*) and I separated, my "one big, happy family" dream was left in the dust as a new reality set in. At thirty-three years old, I found myself alone, angry, and scared with three children, the youngest two years old, as I entered single parenthood. Any textbook on the topic will tell you that the eldest child, my then seven-year-old daughter, was in for a disproportionate load of the emotional burden. Of course, this was unintentional. Carrie was the joy of our lives. She was the first baby who taught us the miracle of life. Carrie was the easiest, most delicious little baby girl imaginable. As I write this, she is now married and six months pregnant. Her pregnancy has been the happiest focal point of the summer.

My former husband, D, and I have buried the hatchet over the last few years and now have a pleasant, at times a bit odd, relationship. He has suggested with a smile that I buried the hatchet in his back, but I know that he is just projecting. I have been happily remarried for close to a decade to my new David, and D has moved on with his life. I thought that it might be time for a symbolic gesture from both of us to our first child, the child of the storm. Maybe it would be meaningful to her if we, as her parents, could buy a gift for her first born that represented unity, hope, and the joy of birth and family. The first thought that came to mind was a crib, the same gift my parents bought for us when Carrie was born. At the time, I didn't realize that this need for an immediate gesture was a strange behavioral form of coping. It was also a good distraction that transformed my fear of surgery into an immediate, tangible expression of love.

For any new grandparent, you have already learned that there is no such thing as a basic crib. Baby furniture is big business now, with convertible crib to full-size headboard pieces, handcrafted dressers and end tables, solid wood with tongue and groove fittings, soft-close drawers and specially fitted mattress sheets. My eyes popped out of my head at the complexity, and this was only the beginning of the drama.

D and I picked one day to accomplish this goal. The upfront challenges included polar opposite styles and tempos around shopping, two college graduations to juggle, busy work schedules, and yes, my bowel prep. As it turned out, the only day that worked for the crib shopping was the one right before my surgery. To anyone with a shred of common sense, this was clearly a set-up for disaster. My daughter and son-in-law, Erin, needed their time to look, discuss, and select their choice. D and I needed to have some part in the process in addition to the check writing, and time was running short. I was hearing the ticking in my head—tick, tock, tick, tock.

I consider myself a high-caliber problem solver and, by nature, a practical sort of person. They are skill sets that I take pride in and no doubt were sharply honed during my single mom years. But somehow, that part of my brain had flipped to standby as we encountered hurt feelings around the shopping dance, difficulty with boundary setting around the scope of the gift, tongue biting with respect to exactly how much furniture could comfortably fit into a ten-by-twelve-foot room. Did you know that twin beds are out? This beautiful grandchild of mine will be spending lots of time playing on top of her lovely full-sized bed—because there won't be any room left on the floor!

Our shopping day arrived, and time was running tight. Laura, my younger daughter, had graduated with her physician assistant degree that morning, and everything seemed so hurried. Hours later I was still choked up from the ceremony and felt apprehensive about infringing on the joy I was feeling with a compressed, emotionally charged shopping expedition. I also knew that bowel prep consumption had to be squeezed in. After all, surgery was scheduled for 7:30 AM the next morning.

Of course, we arrived at the store late, and I ended up ducking into the car to drink the hideous bowel prep cocktail. I went back into the so-called crib store wondering when my stomach would start churning. Carrie was near tears with indecision as she reviewed the endless choices, but D and I remained patient and supportive. After an hour, I thought it best to give her a big hug, leave the decision in her hands, and remind her how much I loved her. I jumped in the car and sped home for fun and games in the bathroom.

On the ride home, alone in the car, I laughed at myself for creating the unnecessary craziness. It seemed like I was in such a panic to squeeze in all the love I could that I was blind to the many simple solutions. As I drove alone, those solutions slowly occurred to me. Instead of the chaos I created, we could have helped them out with a check toward some furniture and let them shop alone. Or better yet, we could have created the symbolic gesture of unity with a pretty sterling silver rattle. It would have been engraved with a short, heartfelt message from the two of us.

Jane and Carrie, 1980

The Sewing Tsunami

I look at my children's bulging closets and can't get over how buying patterns have changed in just one generation. The clothing possibilities are now endless, with a garment's half-life seemingly one to three wears. The premium on designer brands is endemic in the culture. I often find myself reflecting on how it was when I was younger.

To no one's surprise, my family's values around clothing were simple and practical during my childhood years. There were no extra garments. No duplicates in alternate colors and patterns. Everything had a purpose: school clothes, play clothes, dress coat, snow jacket, and snow boots. There were never more than the minimum required quantity of each. No waste. Needless to say, we never ran out of closet space.

When I hit my middle school years and fashion became a higher priority for me, a new struggle began in my home. The London mod scene was in full swing with its colorful fashion statements, and I was starting to panic about showing up at school every day as a plain Jane in my mundane, small collection of school clothes. My blossoming social life required a full array of hip clothing, but in my house, options were limited.

I attended middle school during the 1960s, when home economics, cooking, and sewing were mandatory classes for the girls. Being a craft-oriented child, I found this outlet creative and purposeful. In my school, girls started out learning to sew a sex-role, stereotyped apron, but projects quickly transitioned to jumpers, shirts, blouses, and dresses. The grand finale was a pants suit, back then a new fashion trend! My sewing skill became the pathway to my expanded wardrobe.

My father, with his keen eye for practicality, saw this sewing skill as a solution to my nonstop begging for new outfits. He knew that it took a fair amount of time to properly construct a garment, and the net cost of a homemade outfit was far less than one off the rack in the local department store. So, seeing an opportunity to appear the clever hero and supporter of practical solutions, he grandly declared that as long as I sewed my own clothing, I had a blank check to buy fabric and the other accessories, such as patterns, thread, zippers, and the buttons necessary to complete each item.

So began the sewing tsunami. During the summer months at the lake when I was not swimming or boating, the Ping-Pong table on the porch was converted into a vast sewing table. Shopping trips to the sewing department at Britts, the only department store for miles, became a regular outing. They knew us by name and greeted us with suggestions. I collected an ample supply of patterns and fabric of every sort. I became such a prolific seamstress that, over the course of a summer, I made many dresses, a suit (with bound buttonholes no less), tops, bathing suits, shorts, and pants. I even began to make clothing for my mother. I remember sewing a slinky, black-and-white print halter dress that she kept at the lake for date nights with Pop. Over the years, the clothes transitioned from innocent calico fabrics to Indian prints as we moved into the later 1960s and I became a flower child. My father, who never liked playing the fool, said that if he had any idea how prolific my sewing would become, he would have taken back his generous offer. But being a man of his word, he let this hobby play out and enjoyed the fact that his daughter had become so accomplished at making her own clothing.

By the time I hit college, my mother's old 1940s Singer machine had more mileage than it was ever designed for. I learned how to take it apart and repair it myself. Later, after I had my second child, my parents bought me a new Singer, complete with zigzag stitching and buttonhole features. But my heart stayed true to my first machine. To this day, it remains in my closet, one that barely has enough room for all my store-bought clothes.

The sewing tsunami reminds me to look for creative solutions. Even though new ideas are not always apparent, they can be hiding, like hidden pictures. When we find them, new options come along. As with the sewing, for me those solutions create a personal sense of accomplishment, inner peace, and coming to terms with the unknown.

An Early Lesson in Loving Life

I didn't grow up with computers, the Internet, DVDs, VCR tapes, calculators, cell phones, video games, and satellite radio like my children did. In my house, we had a land line telephone, black and white television with four channels, radio, books, and newspapers. During my childhood years, education and knowledge were transmitted at a slower, less hectic pace. It seemed as if there was much more discussion, especially during dinner. Except for Saturday nights, we always ate dinner together. I had a clear idea of where my parents stood on most worldly and local issues, and their opinions carried a lot of weight. For some reason, that doesn't seem to be the case today. Perhaps the shift is due to the multiple sources and speed of information constantly impacting our children.

In my parents' generation, life was even more simplified and narrow, and that was reflected in their school as well. In Brooklyn during the 1930s, youngsters were taught that memorization was the key to a strong mind. At my elementary school in the mid 1960s, memorization was reserved for multiplication tables and school plays. But at home it was a different story. My parents believed that quickness of mind was achieved through challenge and practice and insisted that we memorize poems (Lewis Carroll's "The Walrus and the Carpenter"), the presidents in order (backward and forward), even a list of facts about the Magna Carta and the Rosetta Stone. Challenges with solving brain teasers, complex math problems, and the meaning of proverbial sayings like "a stitch in time saves nine" filled our dinner table conversations. We all seemed to enjoy the competition. Special verses to memorize were a reward for our accomplishments. And so it was with one of John F. Kennedy's eulogies.

For those of us old enough to remember his assassination, it was as if time froze for the day. For me it was a visceral moment stamped permanently in my memory. I vividly recall my fifth-grade teacher Miss B leaving the classroom and returning moments later in tears. She shared the shocking news and dismissed us for the day. Being a walker, I put on my coat and left for home. My memories from that point on are a blurry set of snapshots filled with video replay of sad scenes on our black and white TV set, days later witnessing the shooting of Lee Harvey Oswald, and rooms of adults crying out for justice.

JFK, born in 1917, was five years older than my father and considered a hero in our home. I'm not sure if it was his service in World War II like my father, his minority status as the first Catholic president, his movie star good looks, or that he had won the death-defying blinking contest during the Cuban Missile crisis. Maybe it was all of that and more, but his death, funeral, and eulogies were discussed, and newspaper stories were read out loud for many days in my home. One eulogy in particular was up for memorization. It was one that my father cut out of the *New York Times,* and he asked my younger brother Leo to master it. Even though Leo was officially asked, we all privately memorized the speech. We knew it was important.

It is now one of the less-remembered eulogies, delivered by a close friend of the Kennedy family. He spoke about the burdens, physical and otherwise, that JFK carried through his life, and the uplifting spirit he shared with his family and country. The most moving part was the ending: "Life was unfair in many ways to John Kennedy. But he never complained; he loved life too much." After digesting the words, complaints about fairness took on a new meaning, and we were always more cautious to use that line of argument.

There is a sad irony that my brother was asked to memorize this passage, because he died so young from cancer. On his final day, he sat on his living room couch with his one-year-old son Brett playing at his feet and his wife by his side. Leo was sick for four years, in and out of treatments and surgery, before he succumbed. He was very private and kept most of his thoughts to himself. He worked until a week before he died. During his last year, Leo periodically called me at work during the day to check in and talk about his son and things he was hoping to get done before his health worsened. I sat listening, thinking about how brave he was. I willed myself to hold onto the sound of his voice, imprinting it into my memory. Strangely, my son Ben has a similar sounding voice, and I catch myself calling him Leo at times. I'm not sure if Leo ever thought about that eulogy while he was ill, but I find myself reflecting on it often. Its meaning resonates in a deep way.

The impact of cancer is hard to capture in words. Most of us surviving it have found it life altering. My first cancer diagnosis almost ten years ago forced me to focus on living in the moment. It made me work harder at taking the higher road in silly conflicts, let go of anger, embrace forgiveness, contribute in more meaningful ways at work, say no sometimes when I would have gone along with the crowd, travel more, and worry less about material things. Most of all, I have learned to take deeper breaths inhaling the essence of my family and friends: their fineness as people, their unique differences, their humor, the occasional disputes, the life lessons we have learned, and the precious time we spend together.

There is always a list of things to complain about, and for certain, life is often unfair. From a distance, through the eyes of a cancer survivor or one who has lost a loved one to the disease, much of it looks pretty trivial. Choosing to love the limited amount of life we are given is a choice implemented with both actions and words and with a deep philosophy of belief in the goodness of every day.

Leo and Jane, 1977

All I Want for Christmas Is
My New Front Teeth

When I was seven years old, I knocked out my two front teeth. It would have been bad enough if they had been baby teeth, but they were my brand new permanent teeth. As it was, they were so pronounced that any orthodontist would have salivated thinking about the costly braces they would eventually need. And if I hadn't knocked them out back then, they would have needed to be dragged across half my face to finally sit in a reasonably humanlike position. They were sitting ducks waiting for an accident to happen.

I didn't have the good luck to knock them out at the same time; it was just my fate to lose them one at a time, one in the fall and one in the spring, just like my cancers. Both accidents involved bicycles (something helmets, by the way, would not have prevented). The first happened at my friend Carol's house when we were walking our bikes up a sidewalk. The bike hit a raise in the asphalt, and my forward-leaning head connected with the handlebar. The second took place while our family was visiting friends on Long Island. I had borrowed a bike and joined the older children for a ride. Unfamiliar with operating hand brakes, I struggled helplessly with my pedals to slow the bike as it began to accelerate down a hill. Moments later, I was propelled over the handle bars and landed on the road. After a mild concussion, a bit of road rash, and losing yet another front tooth, I had to face the reality that my body was no longer perfect.

In a very odd attempt to help me see some humor, I heard lots of comments at home like "Wow, can she ever whistle," "Her teeth are like the stars, they come out at night," and "All she wants for Christmas is her two front teeth." My mother wisely put the kibosh on it. For me the teasing was a little hurtful, but my main concern was the eventual mocking I anticipated at school. I had seen it with other children, and I did not want to become the victim.

Concern was an understatement. I was obsessed with finding a solution to my missing teeth that no one, not even my teachers at school, could detect. I was particularly afraid of the girls who could take simple mockery to an abusive level. When it came to my teeth, my motto was "trust no one." That was the year that I learned to appreciate my right to privacy.

My dentist, a frustrated artist, got busy preparing removable dentures that seemed to grow with my mouth. Looking back at photos from the time, they looked quite good and certainly never kept me from smiling. There were a few close calls in high school when tongues got tangled and the denture came loose, but I managed to somehow recover and avoid an embarrassing confrontation. Shortly after college, a creative orthodontist saw an interesting challenge and came up with a great solution. His plan involved moving my entire bite into a new position by using my lateral teeth as new front teeth. After a little reshaping and bonding, I had some reasonably natural-looking teeth.

From the time I was eight years old until the orthodontic and cosmetic work was finished at age twenty-six, I really did learn to cope with the misfortune, stay open to solutions, and move on. I even chose to be a speech pathologist in my first career. That got somewhat tricky during the dental work, but I made it through somehow. Once the transition was complete, I was delighted to be rid of the denture and functioning with my very own teeth. Until the last few years, my teeth drama stayed a closely guarded secret. I suppose that along the way, I must have outgrown the need for the secrecy, but the memory of school-age girls in particular and their unspeakable cruelty stayed with me. Over time, I grew accustomed to the privacy and coping with some hard stuff alone.

I Thought His Name Was Sven,
But It Probably Was Shlomo

I never looked like a Jewish girl, or what I thought Jewish girls looked like. My outward appearance from the start was a towhead with greenish hazel eyes. As I matured, I grew tall and through most of my life I was somewhat slim with average-sized features. Throughout my childhood and adult years, most people assumed I was Nordic, German, or from some part of the globe that bred people of that Christian appearance.

My parents rejected mass produced traditions, except celebrating Thanksgiving and birthdays; because my Christian friends in my predominantly non-Jewish town were all I had, I understood the ways of non-Jews far better than those of my "chosen" people. My childhood occurred when singing Christian holiday songs and reciting the Lord's Prayer every morning in the public school was the norm, not the exception. I sang in the choir and knew no Jewish music. I played with, flirted with, and dated non-Jewish boys. I later married one. Our eventual divorce had nothing to do with our religious differences. After all, I had become a chameleon, blending in almost perfectly with the Christian community and somewhat less comfortably with the Jewish one. The only blonde in a household of brunettes, people often questioned where those blonde genes came from. I always figured it was the result of some hanky panky in the wheat fields with a guy named Sven many generations back.

My parents grew up in a Jewish community in Brooklyn, but their homes were not ritually observant. My mother's family was more closely aligned with the temple, but she received no formal education.

My father, a product of a terribly harsh divorce during his late youth in the Depression years, had virtually no religious education, and his interest in the Judaism was always at arm's length. Still, he was instinctively protective, even aggressively so, when it came to anything having to do with Israel. This reaction was likely connected to the horrors of the Holocaust and his years as a soldier in World War II. But spiritual matters were viewed with sarcasm and contempt. Except for Yom Kippur and Rosh Hashanah, when we were kept home out of respect for other, more religious Jews and to make a silent statement to our Christian neighbors, there was no real rhythm to the religious seasons. We did not own a menorah or mezuzah. The closest thing to talks with God took place after dangerous close calls, and Pop would glance upward, shake his fist, and say, "Ha, you almost got me again!" He probably would have made a great Israeli soldier as long as he was never asked to pray.

My mother's attempt at our Jewish education consisted of exposing us to a book called *My Neighbor Celebrates* that was written for Christians to help them understand the culture around their Jewish neighbors. It became my reference book and the authoritative source for my Jewish education. Since many of my parents' friends were Jewish, I did learn some Yiddish expressions, mostly dirty, and picked up a little about the religion and culture by osmosis. It really wasn't until college and later that I began to find myself drawn to other Jewish young adults and made some incredibly powerful Jewish friendships of my own.

During my grade school years, being a minority and having a lack of formal Jewish education didn't seem to make much of a difference to me. I was near the top of my class and a fairly good athlete, and since I was a little early to bloom in adolescence, the boys took an immediate interest. But occasionally, I did have to learn the hard way about anti-Semitism, since off-color cracks about Jews were made freely in my presence. With confusion and hurt feelings, I began to resent the ignorance. But knowing practically nothing about my own religion, I was not equipped for an immediate rebuttal and ended up silently carrying away my hurt.

Probably the worst of these experiences took place in fourth grade when my teacher, Miss S (described later by my mother as a "menopausal nut job"), asked me and a classmate Anne to stand up in class. She then announced to the class, "Jane and Anne are Jews." Anne, who it turns out wasn't Jewish at all but Greek, promptly corrected her and was asked to sit down. So, Miss S, in her misguided efforts, instructed me to enlighten the class on what Judaism was all about. Standing alone, I was asked to explain what Jews believed. I was speechless and getting fidgety. She narrowed the question and asked who my God was. I mumbled something about Moses, the first and only Biblical name that came to mind. Seemingly satisfied with my answer, she let me sit down. Fortunately, she knew less than I did. I told my parents about this story years later when I came home from college one vacation. My mother was surprised that I never shared this awful event with her. Although it wasn't her nature to make waves, she was furious with this teacher for humiliating me. Looking back, I'm not sure why I never told her.

A few years after my fourth-grade incident, my younger brother was cornered at school by a pack of Italian boys around Easter who aggressively accused him of killing Christ. He had a much cooler head than I did, and he said casually, "So, turn me in" and walked away. They never bothered him again.

So today, I find my genetic mutation, one that surprised me with breast cancer ten years ago and primary peritoneal cancer now, an ironic twist of fate and even more so, a peculiar reminder of the connection to my ancient Jewish heritage. I think about the hundreds of times over my life that Jews and non-Jews have said, "You're Jewish? You sure don't look Jewish" with surprise in their voices, and can't help but now scoff. My father used to tell me that to be Jewish meant being singled out to stand on the line that led to the gas chamber. No Nazi cared about whether you went to shul, if one parent was Jewish and one not, the shape of your nose, or what color your eyes and hair were. He sounded pretty harsh, but I understood his point that the observance of faith was never the defining point for Jews. What I did not understand, nor did he at that time, was that the many centuries of forced clans or shtetls that Jews lived in would also define our heritage through the slow evolution of fragile cells carrying a heightened risk of cancer.

My Sister Ann

My mother read to us often. She was a perfect role model of the parent who took time to read to her children, and it is a strong, deeply imprinted memory. One of our early favorites was a book of poetry by A. A. Milne, *Now We are Six*. It just so happened that in that book of poems, one seemed to be written for me and one for my sister Ann. Hers was titled "Buttercup Days":

> Where is Anne?
> Head above the buttercups,
> Walking by the stream
> Down among the buttercups.
> Where is Anne?
> Walking with her man,
> Lost in a dream,
> Lost among the buttercups ...

Just my luck, and a perfectly accurate description of how polar opposite we were, my poem, "The Good Little Girl", had to do with behavior:

> It's funny how often they say to me, "Jane?
> "Have you been a good girl?"
> "Have you been a good girl?"
> And when they have said it, they say it again,
> "Have you been a good girl?"
> "Have you been a good girl?" ...

Ann and I were born six months and fifteen days apart. I was the surprise pregnancy that came six years after my mother was told she would not be able to conceive, and Ann was the infant they adopted and brought home at four days old from Brooklyn Hospital. Around the same time Ann was born, my mother realized she was pregnant. My parents saw this as a much unexpected gift and quickly prepared for raising two babies very close in age, eventually sharing the same year in school.

We were both healthy, bright children. That was about where the similarities ended. I was blonde, and Ann brunette. I was a tomboy who loved climbing trees and throwing a ball. Ann was a sweet, gentle child often found playing with her dolls. I tended to be competitive, pensive, and argumentative. Ann was agreeable and had a natural manner for charming others. I was neat; she was sloppy. I spent years figuring out a career path. Ann always knew that she would be a nurse. The differences were endless and still are.

Sometimes I wonder what keeps us glued together. Was it sharing a bedroom, first cribs, and then our twin beds? Was it all of those wonderful lake home days when we explored and lost ourselves in nature's endless imaginary games? Was it that we shared parents and a family? Did we have a silent bond of secrecy and trust to help us cope with those rebellious teenage years? Was it the many inside jokes of our unique home that only we could fully understand? Was it the tragic loss of our younger brother, Leo, later in life that we both felt so deeply? Or was it simply a sister thing, that all-encompassing familiarity that comes from experiencing early life together?

Now in our fifties, we live far apart and share occasional phone calls. We are as different now as we have always been. But when I had my first cancer surgery ten years ago, Ann came to take care of me. She combined her early interest in alternative treatments with a careful eye on my conventional medicine, and I felt safe in her healing touch. She stayed with me at the hospital and almost never left my side. This time around, with two smart, compassionate daughters, both practicing physician assistants, and a medical world that now embraces complementary medicines, I turned down her offer. I knew that Ann had her hands full at home, and I was more concerned about our mother needing her support.

But she found a uniquely "Ann way" to reach me. She knew the express lane that led deep into our common past and my heart. It came in a package of soft, healing items with a most beautiful handwritten card containing a poem much like the ones from our childhood. It made my tears flow.

Jane,
Remember when we were small,
gliding through the lily pads
catching the flowers in our hands.
I love you,
Ann.

Ann, I love you too.

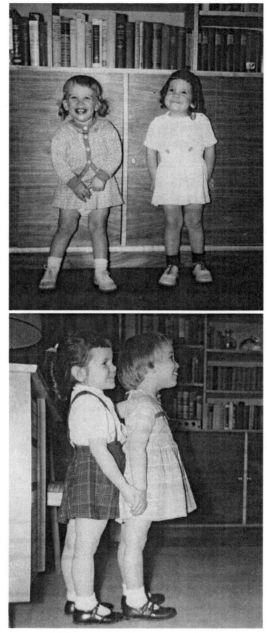

Gilda, Ann and Jane, 1954-1955

Here Comes the Sun

"Here comes the sun, here comes the sun, and I say it's alright."
—The Beatles

It was the fall of 1967, my first year of high school. Powerful changes were in the air. The Vietnam War was in full force and high school boys were talking about registering for the draft, deferment, or leaving for Canada. There was a background drone of liberated behavior in Haight Ashbury and the East Village in New York, and the suggestion of drugs was constantly around us. Hair was getting longer and the generational divide at home and high school was quickly widening.

For the first time, I was among older teenagers, and I found the age spread exciting and distracting. I was noticing the boys, and they were looking back at me. My mind and body were on fire, but I was clueless about sex, drugs, and rock 'n roll. I was spinning in my adolescent chaos. Who was I anyway? Was I among the brainiacs of the school, the jocks, or was I morphing into a flower child? Clearly, I had elements of each, and although the first two were more familiar ground, the call of the wild and urge to explore began to overwhelm me. Sure my folks, or should I say my mother, who viewed herself as open-minded on the topic of sex, had told me about reproduction and birth control, but it was with the cross-sectional female views of a biology book. The word orgasm was never mentioned, and since only female organs were shown to me, I had never seen any pictures of a penis at rest or otherwise. So, although I understood the mechanics and the biology behind making babies, I had no idea about the power of hormones, the helpless sensation of succumbing to the touch of a boy-man, or the emotional entrapments connected to love. I had never experimented with drugs either; I didn't even know their names and had never smoked a cigarette.

I was on the cusp of change. I was about to learn much more than history and algebra for the next four years. The music of the time became a background soundtrack and has long since become a foundational part of my wiring. The musicians were narrating my story and leading me to the next discovery and adventure. My Beach Boys, Herman's Hermits, Donovan, and Monkeys albums from middle school were replaced with the Beatles, Frank Zappa and the Mothers of Invention, Janis Joplin, Joanie Mitchell, Richie Havens, and the Doors. Their music told the story of rebellion, personal freedom, and the power to move the establishment set in place by our parents.

By my sophomore year, it was common for me to join friends on a weekend evening by a local bus stop, hop on the Lakeland Bus #77, and surreptitiously slip into New York City for the evening. We would weave our way down to the East Village to hear up-and-coming artists play at the Fillmore East and some of the smaller clubs like the Village Gate. Seeing the Doors playing at Madison Square Garden was a life-changing experience for me. I would come home from these secret excursions feeling empowered and older. As I slipped into bed later in the evening, I felt like the home I had known my whole life had gotten smaller, my bedding too juvenile, and the atmosphere stifling.

During these years, I began to discover the artist within. I was a strong believer that there is creativity in all of us, and my outlets of expression were music, drawing, and crafts. I struggled to learn to play the guitar on my own using the years of piano lessons to help me read the music. My fingertips were first raw and then eventually calloused as I learned cords and songs of that day. The walls of my room were covered in band posters and artwork I had bought or created. Big, clumsy headphones were attached to my turntable so that I could listen to music and drown out the sounds of suburban family life. It strikes me as very interesting that now, with such a serious disease on my plate, I once again turn to creative outlets of expression.

The only hitch in this great fantasy was my parents, particularly Pop, who was highly agitated at the realization he was losing control. Now fifty-seven myself and having raised teenagers, I know the bewilderment they must have felt as I slipped out of their grip. But I still cringe when I remember his distrustful treatment of any boy I brought home. I would first march the victim up to Pop's office. He would peer over his glasses and caustically ask, "Who are you?" His tone actually said, "Who the Hell are you?" Predictably, within a date or two or three, Pop would find some minor infraction of the house rules and forbid me to see the poor guy again. Pop became legendary in my high school, a Goliath calling out for a challenge with a testosterone-ridden young man.

Eventually, the fateful day came when Pop pushed too far. I started dating a very exciting boy who was two years older than I. Within a month, Pop found his reason to forbid me to see him. I decided that enough was enough and continued the relationship in secrecy for close to two years. My skill at deception sharpened to a fine art, and I saw the boy regularly, even after he left for college. Eventually, the romance faded and the relationship came to its natural end. I think we both were relieved. Through that I learned that behaving out of spite generally led nowhere good.

Not too long after my secret romance ended, I began to date my first husband, D, someone I had known since we were first graders. He was always a great student and friendly face, and my parents gave in and shared their blessing with me so that we could turn the page and move on to brighter days as a family. I was drunk with the freedom that came with an open, honest relationship with my folks and had a wonderful time winding up high school together with the boy who became my very closest friend and first husband. Even seeing him now, years past our divorce, I find myself surprised by the rush of familiarity and bond from those late adolescent years spent together.

I Never Lived in My
Childhood Home Again

I will be forever grateful to my mother, Gilda, for her determination to ensure I had the opportunity to attend a great college. She finished high school shortly after the Depression when her family was struggling financially to get back on their feet. They needed her to contribute to the household after high school, so she was briefly sent to secretarial school and quickly added another income. Later, her two sisters went to Brooklyn College to become teachers, but by then, Gilda was married to my father and helping him through his postwar schooling. One of her greatest contributions to her children was her commitment to help each of us reach our academic potential. Once again, she demonstrated her strength as the mortar in our family's life.

We discussed many different colleges, and Mom became convinced that if I could swing a way to be accepted at the University of Michigan (U of MI) that was where I should go. As it turned out, my high school academic performance had been a bit lackluster, so I ended up applying to Michigan's nursing college and got into U of MI through a back door.

If high school was an awakening for me, college was where I grew up. My first week on campus was the hardest to get through, and the period from which I have the most vivid memories. Unlike my children who had time to visit colleges and attend early orientations, I had never seen the Michigan campus until I arrived there for school, three days before classes began. My mother and I drove together at the end of the summer of 1971 covering the 630 miles between my old and new life. Pop, who traveled constantly in his work, was quick to back out of the trip and trusted that we capable women would handle things just fine.

There was no early orientation or registration for me, and I was thrown into lines of thousands of students attempting to register for fall classes. More than ten years before desktop computers, registration was accomplished manually with class cards. Close to half a day passed standing on lines, often being told once I reached the front that the class I hoped to take was already full. By noon, I was a wreck, sitting on a bench in tears wondering if I was in over my head. Was this college decision a big mistake? D, who had also decided to attend Michigan, stopped in and gave me a shoulder to cry on. Charitably, he helped me through the rest of the process. It was a big lesson in humility. Just three days earlier, I left New Jersey thinking I was the big deal, heading off to a nationally respected university. In under a week, I learned that I was just another student on a forty-thousand-plus student campus and only another face in the crowd.

Back at the dorm, things weren't much better. My folks, probably with good reason, had insisted I live in an all girls dorm. Co-ed housing was new back then, and my father did not have much faith in it. So, I looked at the map and selected a small dorm close to campus. That was fine until I met my roommate. The girl was an emotional disaster. From a highly conservative family, she had gotten herself involved in a love affair with her married high school German teacher following the sudden death of her father that summer. I was totally ill-equipped and, selfishly, not terribly interested in making her my new best friend. To top it off, our room was the size of my current walk-in closet, outfitted with a bunk bed, two desks, and two dressers. There was nowhere to walk without stumbling over each other. We were both very unhappy. Within a week, I requested a move to a large female-only dorm on the other side of campus, and she managed to convince the resident director to convert her room into a single, win-win.

Finally set up with my class schedule and in a dorm with beautiful architectural touches from the 1920s, I had secured a base of operations. Understanding that I was starting on the bottom of the pile, I began to explore the campus, make friends, and get to my classes. John Lennon performed on campus that year, and Nixon's historic visit to China signaled a new era in international relations. It also was the last year of the Vietnam draft. Although the campus drama of the late sixties was over, there was still a strong sense of political excitement in the air. I began to feel the distance growing between my new life and the one I had left behind.

By the end of the first semester, I developed a good strategy for studying, a skill I had never really focused on before, and a plan for transferring to the larger College of Literature, Science, and Arts (LS&A) program. I once again joined the mainstream of students, having learned my first real lesson about finding solutions "outside of the box." I did not really know what I wanted to major in at that time, but could not envision nursing—blood and vomit were two of my least favorite things. I eventually chose speech pathology after leafing through the one-inch-thick course catalogue from A to Z. The decision was somewhat arbitrary, but I found myself enjoying the material and the people I met. Patti, one of my closest friends back then and still now, and I used to duck out of the speech and audiology building for lunch on cold Ann Arbor winter days. We grabbed our coats and ran across the street to a little luncheonette, Angelo's, and had thick, homemade raisin bread toasted with hot melted butter. I later learned how to bake similar bread of my own and often still do on cold, snowy days.

I loved having D in the picture with me, too. Away from our parents and our hometown, we had the freedom to enjoy our relationship and set out on adventures together. Like two peas in a pod, we navigated our freshman year, found a way to stay on campus for summer classes, and moved into off-campus housing. We became inseparable.

Lenny Bruce Co-op was my next home. To me, it was a very hip and progressive place to live. Housing close to sixty students, we saved rent money by participating in purchasing groups and maintained the house by arranging cooking and cleaning schedules. We bought organically grown food from local farms. In the backdrop were the Watergate hearings. I worked part time at the graduate library and remember coming home in the early evening to lively discussions about the treacherous nature of Washington politicians. There were many fascinating students who lived there. It was our nonconformist attempt to offset the dominant Greek life on the campus. We just created our own subculture. Thanks to Facebook, I have even rediscovered my roommate from that year.

By my junior year, D and I were eager to live together and take a number of road trip adventures. Our parents were vehemently opposed based on moral grounds. So one rainy day, sitting beside him in his old blue Volvo, he turned to me and asked if I would marry him. We were only nineteen and neither of us had more than a nickel to our name. Although at the time I saw this as a pretty risky move, I was in love and could not see myself with anyone but him. Always the pragmatist, I figured that we would wait years for children. This would give us the room to explore together, and years later, we would be ready for a family. So much for sensible planning ...

We remained in Ann Arbor for eight years and completed our undergraduate degrees, my graduate degree in Speech and Language, and D's medical school. During that time, we lived in three different apartments, getting a view of the town and campus from every angle. We backpacked in Europe twice and drove out West for extended camping trips several times. When we weren't studying or traveling, we were worrying about money. Although we both worked during those years, money was always very tight and seemed to be the lightening rod of most of our disputes. Neither one of us saw the fault line that was growing between us. In spite of it all, we packed up for St. Louis, me pregnant and preparing to enter my second graduate program in business administration. D was entering his surgical internship and residency at Washington University. We had grown up without even realizing it. Like the pioneers long gone, I felt the need to head West, or should I say Midwest, explore, and set out on my own. After close to a decade away, I knew that it was too late to turn back. I don't remember even considering it.

Rhodes, Greece, 1975

You Know It's Over When ...

Divorced people often try to pinpoint when they first realized their marriage was over. On a ski vacation years back, some man told me while riding up the ski lift that he knew it was over when he trapped his wife under the covers after a particularly spicy meal and made her stay under there, while he filled the airspace with his flatulence. As he recounted the story, he was stunned by his own lack of remorse at her near hysteria. Although I laughed at his tale, I could not share my moment; it was far too personal to me.

Now, more than twenty years since my first marriage ended, I can recount the moment I knew things were over between D and me without feeling pain. I don't think about those times much anymore, but years back I was constantly obsessing about them. Marriages rarely end because of only one reason or one person's wrongdoing, and that was true of mine. It took years of slow, emotional erosion to hit that trigger point where we could no longer sustain our connection to each other. There were lots of hints along the way, but I chose to minimize their importance. Perhaps I shouldn't have.

The day the insight hit me was a couple of years before our divorce, the day our third child Ben was born. Having had two intimate experiences in the labor and delivery rooms with our daughters' births, I expected another heartfelt experience. Excited about having a son, and after a scare with bleeding in the tenth week of pregnancy, I was full of anticipation. We knew he was going to be a large baby and that it might take a little work to deliver him. However, going into the hospital already well dilated made things move along unexpectedly fast.

It was my first experience in a birthing room, and I was much more relaxed in that environment. D settled into a chair by the window with a stack of professional journals expecting a long labor. He barely looked up at me. For the most part, the nurses helped me with my breathing and coached me through one hour of labor. Suddenly, I was ready to push. My body had moved quickly into high gear.

I looked over at my husband reading. He seemed to be in a private space, totally detached from me and others in the room. I kept looking over hoping to catch his eye. After a few minutes of watching this, the nurses interrupted him and politely suggested that he come over and help. I was annoyed and embarrassed that he seemed so disinterested. Quickly the contractions and pushing upstaged all else. Minutes later, Ben was born; a beautiful little boy, with a shock of red hair, weighing eight pounds and nine ounces.

I watched D take Ben in his arms and look into his son's eyes with love. He walked around the room a few times radiating excitement. A few minutes later, he gently handed him to me, but there was no kiss, hug, or words of affection. I looked into his face with anticipation, but he turned away. After that point, my memory became a blur as it slowly began to dawn on me that I was going to be facing an impossible uphill battle to save my marriage.

Single and Scared

I have always had a lot of pride. Although reportedly one of life's deadly sins, I believe it was also a motivating force propelling me through the harder times of my life. Never wanting to be a victim or the pitied topic of others' dinner table conversations, I tried to hold my head up high as I redesigned my personal and family life. But underneath the cool exterior, I was terrified.

Holding my head up high was not always easy to do. Somewhat of a dreamer, I had imagined a Camelot-like existence: a home filled with happy children, and my husband and I prospering in our careers and interests. So the reality of facing single life with my three children, ages two, five, and seven, was daunting. Unfortunately, the divorce was far from amicable during its first few years. Money was in short supply, for me at least, and the children and I were in a tailspin. It was also clear that in order to fill in the financial gaps I would need to get my tired, highly educated self back into the workplace. I had taken two years off to be home after the birth of Ben, my third child, my non-sleeper, and the heightened emotions around the divorce left me feeling insecure about my skills and overall worth.

Within a year, with the support of family and friends, I began to pull myself back together and was once again employed. But I needed to restrain my Type A personality as I compared myself to women my age moving upward past me into more significant leadership roles. There was no way for me to add more to the day. Balancing the needs of three very active children, working, and attempting dating was all I could handle in a twenty-four-hour day. Work was put into a coasting mode for a number of years so that I could focus on my family and developing new friendships. Dating is a tale in its own right.

It was not always stressful. The story of my children and me during that early era is also full of love, adventure, and learning. They were my anchor and motivation to pull myself back together. I knew I needed to redesign a stronger, different structure for them to grow within, but I wasn't sure what it should look like. So I learned as they grew. My top priority was to keep the family together in a way that made our little group of four feel complete, secure, and full of happy memories. I wasn't always successful with those goals, but they were important to me, and I often made hard choices to keep our little boat on course.

Back then, our house seemed like a dream, bigger than I could ever afford without a good job. So I found employment that would provide greater financial security. With three children, day care was far too expensive, and with their five year age spread their social and emotional needs were all different. So, I hired nannies to help at home. The nanny experience was at times excellent and, at other times, simply terrible. The nannies were all young and several had special needs of their own. Two were sent home after only a week, both with alcohol problems. Several had not outgrown their teenage antics, and from time to time, I was parenting them as well, including taking the extra car away. I felt cheated at times, not being home for important moments or for ordinary ones like baking cookies. The worst day I can remember was when I forgot Ben's Halloween costume. I was in a panic to get everyone to school and myself off to work that day. Something I can no longer remember was brewing in the office. His kindergarten teacher called me up after lunch, way too late to fix the problem. She scolded me on the phone, accusing me of being neglectful. I put my head down on the desk and cried. The second worst day was when I missed parent appreciation night at his high school soccer game. I think I was away on a trip. After a few of those mistakes, I tried hard to remember to always put the children ahead of both work and men.

Realizing that every family has its own unique chemistry, I tried hard to find a style that worked for us. Initially, it was time after work and on the weekends. Once home for the evening, I took over. Checking remaining homework, reading, and unwinding were important to me. We had one TV set in the family room, and it was reserved for special shows and video tapes. It was not constantly on, and the kids didn't seem to care. On my therapist's advice, I took turns at bedtime, going room to room, giving each child my undivided attention. They learned to respect the system and waited their turns. Ben, being the youngest, came first. He was a bundle of thinly controlled energy (later a dynamite athlete) and generally fell asleep quickly. We made up games with his Curious George stuffed animal, and for years, I think he was convinced they were all real. At the end of each game, George was tired and put his head on the pillow. Ben always followed suit. One night after he was punished for taking money from Carrie, he was sent to his room early and told to go to bed. When I checked in later, I found him face down on his bed with a note hanging out of his pajama bottoms. It said, "I'm sorry, Mom. Can I have a back rub now?" In spite of his constant antics, Ben found a way to communicate his very simple needs in such an irresistible way.

Laura, three years older than Ben, came next. She was also imaginative and loved to create stories. Her favorite theme was centered on the wooded area behind our house. Laura had a natural affinity to wildlife; she loved the deer and other small animals. In our stories, she became a beautiful princess with a wreath of flowers in her hair, riding on the back of a deer and saving the lives of smaller animals. Sometimes we made up alliterations using the first letter of her name: "In a little loft lived a lovely girl named Laura who was very lively and licked lollipops." We usually ended up in giggles, often making Carrie very impatient for her turn. Laura was also at an age when night terrors were common. Routinely, she would race into my room in the middle of the night, crying and jumping onto my bed. Dead tired, I would break the golden rule and let her under the warm covers, and we would both quickly fall back asleep. She used to call it the "magic bed," since all of her nightmares disappeared once she slipped in. So much for my soothing abilities! A year or so later, I bought a new bed for myself and put my old one in her room. I announced to Ben and Carrie that Laura was now the keeper of the magic bed. Her room was the designated location when we needed comforting from nightmares. It's funny how all night terrors seemed to vanish. Sometimes I do see examples of how my father's offbeat sense of humor rubbed off on me.

Laura had a series of guinea pigs, because none seemed to live very long. That didn't seem to stop her from loving each one with every ounce of feeling she had. It was a drizzly day when the first one died. I noticed Laura standing at the end of the driveway in tears waiting for me to come home from work. Panic raced through my body when I saw her outside crying in the rain. Visions of mass murder flashed through my head, and I felt tremendous relief when I realized that the single casualty was a rodent. But when she said through her sobs, "Now I know why everyone was so sad when Uncle Leo died," I quickly realized how love comes in so many unconditional forms, and that it took the loss of a pet for her young mind to realize the gravity of death. Always having a big heart and emotions close to the surface, Laura was quick to make friends. I think that of my children, she inherited Grandma Lily's contagious laugh.

Carrie, my oldest, liked to talk. She would settle back onto her pillow and happily discussed any topic. Sometimes it was school, sometimes issues around the dynamics of the divorce, and often, plans for upcoming weekends and vacations. She always seemed older than her years, and I often made the classic mistake of confiding too much in her. To this day, I wish I had had a better understanding of her need for childhood boundaries, but having had a "tough love" upbringing of my own and with some underhanded divorce dynamics going on, I found it difficult to resist falling into the trap. Always a pleaser, she wanted to make everyone happy, especially me. Her efforts were amazing. She would plan wonderful Mother's Day mornings, treasure hunts on birthdays, and exciting projects. My gifts were typically on the front lawn and required a bathrobe and slippers to retrieve. One of my favorite stories followed a reminiscing of the aquariums that my siblings and I assembled during our childhood lake days. Carrie, a bit of a Pied Piper personality, gathered the local children to help out. Together at the top of the driveway, they built a special exhibit of insects. It was quite impressive and included hand-built shelving full of bugs of every sort: worms, salamanders, spiders, ants, etc. The only hiccup was that she used all of my brand new Tupperware as cages. When I saw the display, I had to take a deep breath and try not to overdo my reaction to the containers. I found the good sense to laugh it off and grabbed my video camera. Carrie's creativity grew as her interests developed. Her pottery, sculptures, photos, and masks decorate my home to this day.

The girls had a favorite game they still enjoy reminding me about. We called it "Bad Barbie." Both girls, unlike their mother, had a passion for playing with their vast Barbie collection. With a far greater affinity for throwing a ball with Ben or trying to teach them all tennis, I succumbed every once in a while to their pleading to play dolls. Over time it became a bit of a special treat because of my outlandish behavior. The only way I could stay engaged was to throw my own spin on the game. I became that naughty girl who just couldn't be polite or play by the rules. My Barbie could not assemble a coordinated outfit or be taken on any outings without acting out and having to be scolded by one of their perfectly attired Barbies. They sat holding their breath for me to start with my antics, and although they made a few feeble attempts to correct me, I was entirely out of control, and we would all end up on the floor laughing. To this day, when any of us, particularly me, is getting impatient in restaurants or with store clerks and letting those inner feelings show, I get an elbow in my side or a whisper in my ear and am reminded to stop acting like a Bad Barbie.

As they entered their school-age years, my itch for family adventure began to grow. I had always imagined taking them out West to see the national parks. Although summer vacations near family at the Delaware beaches were restful and lots of fun, I wanted to make sure that they saw the beauty in our country. Once Ben was old enough to carry his own backpack of toys, we planned our first trip to the Grand Tetons and Yellowstone national parks. Each child had a journal with colored pencils for drawing and writing their observations. We left behind television, movies, and video games and replaced them with hikes, horseback riding, and books at night in our modest cabins. We ate in park mess halls and looked forward to the piping hot oatmeal and pancakes each morning for breakfast, frequently meeting other travelers and sharing ideas for activities. I was immensely proud of them as a little team and felt satisfied that I kept a commitment I had made about my child-rearing philosophy.

Over the next several years, we alternated between beach vacations and more trips to the West. These breaks gave me ample time to collect flight points and keep the trips within my modest budget. Our second Western vacation was a long road trip starting in Phoenix and ending in Denver. One unforgettable episode was our most dangerous family memory. It happened in the Grand Canyon during a mule ride down and up Bright Angel Trail. The ride down was breathtaking and took us to a beautiful landing half way to the bottom where we lunched before heading back. The trails were narrow, with steep drops and short switchbacks. We were reassured by the wranglers that the mules knew their way and were sure footed. Under no circumstances were we to get off of the animals. Once the initial terror of riding down those harrowing trails wore off, we settled into a steady pace, descending several thousand feet to the landing.

After lunch and within a half hour on our ride back up, a monsoon broke through the sky. Hail and driving rain began to pour down the walls of the canyon, showering our heads and bodies with water, rocks, and dirt. We had hats and ponchos but were still getting clobbered with canyon debris and hail. Everyone was terrified. The wrangler, who was riding in the front with Ben and another young boy, had already passed a switchback. All I could see was a waterfall ahead separating them from the group. I looked back to the girls, and their mules had begun to turn around, heading back down the canyon. I turned to follow and gather them, having no idea how to manage my mule but knowing that I didn't want them on their own. When I caught up with them, they were crying with looks of pain and panic on their faces. I could not believe I had so innocently exposed everyone to such danger. I helped them turn their mules around to head back up to the wrangler and Ben. The rain subsided, and we all caught up to each other. Immediately, helicopters began to descend into the canyon looking for victims. It was simply unbelievable and reminded me of towns on TV ravaged by tornados or the aftermath of plane crashes. Another group of wranglers came down the canyon to help. We were asked to dismount. The wranglers led the mules back up the canyon, leaving us to walk through the rubble ahead of them. By that point, the biggest problem was the lack of bathroom facilities. Once at the top, we all raced for comfort.

We were told that the trail was closed for two weeks afterwards, just to clean off the rock that had fallen. We were so lucky to have come through it unharmed. Maybe there were angels on that trail after all. The rest of the trip, Laura, my worrier, was constantly on guard for falling rock. By the end of the vacation, after collecting a lot of fun adventures, we logged it in as a character-building experience that we got through as a family and would never forget. We still talk about it to this day. Fortunately, I did manage to video a discussion later in the evening while we ate dinner. One of these days, I will pull it out and share it with the children.

For all of the hard work it took to raise young children alone, there were immeasurable rewards. The greatest of all is the closeness that I feel with each of them individually and then again as a group. I can see their unity now when problems arise or if an event needs to be planned. Their first phone call is always to each other. That brings tremendous joy and relief knowing their bond will keep them strong, eventually without me.

Carrie, Laura, Ben: August, 1987 –
the summer my first marriage ended

Teenagers and Transitions

Raising teenagers—with it comes so many potential themes: the search for unique identity, rebellion, discovery of the wanting child within, the blame for all wrongs on the out-of-touch adults in their world, and the wistful innocence that they and their generation alone would do it all differently and finally "get it right." There is something remotely familiar sounding about all of that. Wasn't it the same way I felt at their age? Strangely, my compassion for my parents increased exponentially when each child reached thirteen. When I was an impossible teen, Pop used to say, "I should only live long enough to see you have teenage daughters!"

Foolishly, I talked myself into believing that if I used adult reason with each child, I would elicit adult behavior. Clearly, I was way off base. My children, always the closest people to me in my life, insidiously became more distanced, neither reliably honest nor trustworthy. They bewildered me, because just as I was throwing my hands in the air, they all in their time would do something really thoughtful and mature. I was never quite sure if this was part of the adolescent strategy to keep me off balance or the uneven maturation of their teenage brains. I completely forgot my dishonesties as a teenager and the gradual adulthood understanding that dawned on me in my early college years. Somehow, I had deluded myself into thinking that it would be different with my own children. Exactly who was the fool? I now hear the kids boast about the parties they pulled off, and the exploitation of the divorced parents' cracks in supervision as we handed the three of them back and forth. In the end, we all got through it. Thank God for the foundation of unconditional love. Ultimately, I believe that is what glues us together through the ups and downs.

As the children created distance, those years became lonely for me. Teenage friends became far more central in their lives, and I had to rethink my own life goals, especially with their colleges and a geographic distance approaching. Slowly, my ability to restart momentum at work gained traction. Over a few years, some important projects and job changes led me to greener, more rewarding pastures. It was also during those years that I challenged myself to grow in some new directions. I had been lamenting about trips of the past and was ready to harness the courage to travel alone. I had been involved with ensuring numerous travel enrichment opportunities for each child but not for me. Perhaps deep inside, I was yearning for new adventures.

Carrie was an exchange student in Buenos Aires for a summer, and aside from an early exposure to Latin club life, became proficient at Spanish, later having fun with her Argentinean accent in Spanish class. Laura participated in an Outward Bound trip to Belize, helping build signs for the local parks out of gravel and river water. Ben took several Outward Bound trips, one to the Northeast and one to the Northwest. Those experiences helped build confidence, taught them to contribute and appreciate others in a small team setting, and reinforced their love of nature. Now, it was my turn. I began planning a European bike trip.

In addition, I was emotionally spent from a decade of disappointing dating experiences and failed romances. It was time for me to take a hard look at what I was really after in the world of adult love and companionship. I knew that there were some good reasons things weren't going my way beyond the "single woman with three kids" excuse. It was time to focus on my own behaviors and begin charting a new course.

A View from the Other Side of the Drape

It's dark and scary over here on this side of the drape. Could it be a bad dream? Will I wake up in a sweat and feel thankful that my imagination supplanted reality? I think not.

One random morning I woke to find myself on the front line of a personal battlefield. Feeling alone, I was armed with early twenty-first century weapons, a knife, a surgeon's eye, and my oncologist's poisons, the weak weapons of mass destruction. I hoped that my enemy was sleepy or distracted, and I would have an advantage.

I have always worked in health care. My career began thirty-four years ago when I started out as a speech and language pathologist working in a poor, rural school district in Washtenaw County, Michigan. I later took a position at the University of Michigan working with brain-injured adults. In St. Louis, I used my skills to pay for an MBA, combined with a degree in health care administration. My first hospital position was at a mega medical center in St. Louis and marked the beginning of my career as a hospital administrator. A typical baby boomer youngster, I was looking for a helping profession. Speech pathology was an early gamble, and as I worked, I began to refine my direction. But one thing was for sure: I never expected to be on the other side of the drape.

For the last twenty years, I have worked in three different hospital systems in New Jersey. As good fortune would have it, in most cases I was hired to do what I like best, clinical program development. I love taking an idea and turning it into something new, strategic, and tangible. My industry is rapidly expanding with older, sicker patients and continually challenged to find safer, more efficient and cost-effective programs and technologies. A wise mentor once told me that if you keep the patients' needs at the center of your plan, you will not only build the best program, but it will likely work out financially, too. So far, she hasn't steered me wrong. It all comes down to providing the critical level of care with a constant eye on quality.

So, my latest experience as a patient has put me intimately in touch with my consumer, the patients, the sick people. It has forced me over to the other side of the drape, where people need help, get treated, live, and sometimes die.

I was just like any other patient. I wanted the basics: reassurance that I was getting the best care possible, that I would be safe from additional injury to my body, that there would be no avoidable delays in my care, and that my privacy would be safeguarded. We all want and expect that from our doctors and hospitals, and I was no different. If anything, I was on extra good behavior. After all, I wanted to minimize the potential for future stories of any over-the-top antics when I returned to work. The verse from A. A. Milne kept running through my head:

It's funny how often they say to me, "Jane?
"Have you been a good girl?"
"Have you been a good girl?"

For those cancer veterans, you know that it starts with picking the right physicians. As a second timer, and an industry insider, I did have an edge. It was important to me to receive my care close to home, where I knew my family could be available to support me without crossing rivers, sitting in traffic, and getting stressed out. I asked lots of questions and double checked the treatment plan with a couple of renowned cancer centers. My oncologist was always one step ahead and reassured me that those important calls had been made already. When your physicians put your care ahead of their own egos, you know that they have passed a critical professional test and that you are on the right track. It was also great to be spared the wear and tear of traveling around to get more advice. This was a tremendous relief to me. After all, who needs those kinds of field trips when you are already hanging by your nails on the anxiety cliff?

The harrowing workup came next. Most people say that the waiting is the worst part; that even if the news is bad, not knowing is worse. I agree in part. It certainly feels that way at the time, but we all hope and pray that what we are going to hear is manageable. For many of us, the workup includes labs, radiological studies, and a biopsy. The diagnostics were tough for me. I kept thinking, "Don't look down." There is no avoiding it though. Sitting in waiting rooms for studies and procedures and then waiting for results is like being transported into the Jean Paul Sartre play *No Exit*. Wave after wave of anxiety poured over me.

Damn, just when I thought I had outrun this insidious disease, the sky falls. But in spite of it, I continued working, met with my rabbi looking for words of advice and wisdom, and also called my lawyer to update my will. It was impossible for me to just sit around and wait. I had to do something I felt control over. Knitting for my new grandchild just didn't keep me adequately distracted.

I work with surgeons every day and enjoy going down to the OR to look at the processes, equipment, and people at work. I think it is fascinating. Blood doesn't seem to bother me like it once did. On a simplistic level, it is like an ant farm, with everyone looking the same in their scrubs, hats, and gowns. They are constantly moving around, all with a sense of purpose. It is also one of the most dangerous parts of a hospital, where a sudden, unexpected error can create chaos. Once the door to the OR closes, the life of the patient (that would be me) is in the team's hands. So, I worked on making sure I had a team that respected each other's talents and limits. The resident was top notch, and I trusted my surgeon's judgment that the resident's portion of the operation would remain within his skill set.

My surgery was scheduled for a Thursday morning, and I had to be at the hospital at 5:30 AM sharp. Once there, I was ready to bolt right out, but I looked at my husband and children and obediently climbed into the wheelchair. The nurse wheeled me down one floor—almost directly beneath my office. How strange is that? The idea of a stem-to-stern incision was quietly freaking me out. I was worried that more organs were going to be involved, and I would wake up in an ICU with bags hanging out of me. It was all I could do to control my fear. But the nurses knew that patients usually feel this way, and they were reassuring. The anesthesiologist and surgeons went over the plan again, and then quickly started me on some calming medicine. I don't remember much after that point. But I do remember drifting off to sleep, confident that everyone had brought his and her A game.

My son's fiancé, Laura, was an OR nurse at the hospital and kept the family in the loop all morning. Communication is so very important for everyone.

I woke up a few hours later in the post-operative area. I vaguely remember asking the same questions over and over, seeing my families' faces, seeing the chief nursing officer double check that all was in order, and after a while, being brought up to my room. My children had decorated the windowsill by my bed with some of my favorite family pictures. There were roses from my husband and pretty, colorful flowers from my children. It was comforting and made me feel loved. I seemed to be in a deep fog for days, just wakeful enough to talk about my pain. My doctors stopped by to check for anything serious and to say hello, but by this point, most of my care was in the hands of the nursing staff. They are the critical linchpin during recovery. Their diligence in focusing on the subtle signs of trouble can make all the difference for the patient. They look for signs of infection, ensure that the patient is receiving the correct medications, and get the patient up and around and home in the optimal time. They care for, educate, and tune into the emotional uphill climb that every patient experiences after a physical assault, either planned or by accident.

For me, the biggest hurdle was an almost constant state of nausea that was depressing and anchored me to my bed. Eventually, the team, including my physician assistant daughters, figured out a new drug combination and the feeling began to pass. On post-op morning four, I woke up at 5:30 AM and felt like having a real shower and going home. Something inside just clicked, and I knew I was ready. I dragged myself out of my room, attached to my IV pole, and headed to the nurses' station. I asked if I could take a shower before the day shift started. Being obsessed with my weight since I was fourteen, I also wanted to get weighed. After all, I had consumed virtually no calories to speak of in five days and wanted some good news.

The surgical resident turned me down on the shower, but my nurse led me down the hall to the bariatric scale, quite a large apparatus. For those who have never seen one, it is a platform with a bench, large enough to hold me and a few of the smaller nurses. I must have looked like a waif standing on it. I saw the number that came up, and I could not believe it. I had gained five pounds! I glared at the tiny nurse in disbelief and asked if it could possibly be wrong. She looked at me with a smile and reminded me that I had absorbed a lot of fluids, and they would take some time to flush through my body. I glanced down the hall at the nursing team who were experts in bariatric care. I threw my arms out and said, "The surgery was a miracle! Just look at me now!" We all had a good laugh, and I told my nurse that I was going home today. Gaining five pounds after all that I had just endured was the last straw. I wanted to take my shower, collect my stuff, and go home. She patiently nodded and led me back to my bed to wait for the physicians. What a little saint she was! That was my second hissy fit.

My first meltdown came the night before. My family loves to cook and eat together. It is one of our favorite things to do, and we always look forward to sharing each others' company over a nice meal. So, true to form, and also as a coping mechanism to deal with the stress, we reverted to our typical comfort behaviors. The only problem was the head count. At meal time there were typically five to seven people around, and hospital rooms are not designed like restaurants. Wanting to keep everyone happy, because that also made me feel happy, I allowed this to go on meal after meal. But after a few days, a no-nonsense nurse whispered in my ear and reminded me that I was her chief concern. If I was feeling overstimulated, all I needed to do was give her a wink, and she would politely (or otherwise) end the picnic. I was the only one of the group who adored her. Everyone else was afraid. By the last night, as I was becoming lucid, things seemed to be getting more out of hand. My single room, full of emotionally fatigued family, had become the food court, with everyone but me enjoying the varieties of tastes and smells. I finally cracked. My eldest daughter quickly moved everyone to the family waiting area. But my snapping managed to hurt everyone's feelings. After all, they were scared for me and trying so hard to be helpful.

As I reflect on the whole experience, there were parts that deeply moved me and made me connect with others. Physicians, nurses, technicians, and housekeepers shared their empathy and stories. Those stories were all very personal experiences where they or their families faced similar health challenges and somehow conquered them. I am now the keeper of a lot of secrets. There were times when complete strangers held my hand to reassure me. They instinctively knew the great healing power that comes with simple human contact, with touch. And now, when I come back to the hospital for appointments or to visit my staff, the concierge, Danny, a man with a bottomless well of good will, greets me and tells me how wonderful it is to see me back on my feet. The emotional side of healing can never be underestimated. It takes fortitude and strength to face the long climb back, and there is simply no yardstick to measure the power of positive people.

I feel tremendous gratitude to everyone who was involved in my care and many who helped from a distance. They all played a role in keeping me safe, getting the job done, and helping me heal. Through their care, I was able to stay positive in the early days of this cancer journey, when there was a faint line between fear and hope.

The Cancer Etiquette Dance

No one seems to really know how to act around a cancer patient. I'm not sure that as one I'm too clear on it either. What I can say, with the benefit of hindsight, is that it is a delicate dance requiring great sensitivity and perhaps a bit of mind reading. An advanced degree in clinical psychology wouldn't hurt either. As a survivor, I admit that my mood affects what I am comfortable with from others at any given time, but I now realize there are a few ground rules too. In the beginning, I needed to hold onto the reins and take the first moves in my own way.

My first step was telling the immediate family the crummy news. I was most concerned about my mother, as she already had endured the loss of so many loved ones, and I didn't want her frightened. But I also didn't feel strong enough to carry her anxiety on top of mine. So when I did speak to her, I asked her to tell her close friends the news and use my sister (instead of me) to vent to and for daily support. I asked her to keep all discussions with me positive so that I could focus on my treatment and not be worrying about her too. My children were immediately supportive and zeroed in on the business of surgery and chemotherapy. As health care professionals, they had that built-in reflex. My husband, who went through the diagnostic testing with me, always focused on the silver lining. He listened attentively to the physicians and their predictions about the odds of a bad outcome, but he is a glass half full type of guy—that was clear from the day we met. He stayed focused on the chances of good results.

In the beginning, I needed all of my energy to cope or deny, or whatever it was that I was trying to do to shake off the anxiety and figure out how I was going to work through this illness. Like my father, who had to maneuver his WWII B-22 airplane around the dump his monkey took on their navigation map, I had to revise my life course and chart a new flight plan.

My husband, who always liked answering the phone more than I did anyway, took over "communications central." He served as my publicist and shared the few details I was comfortable putting out there, while expressing our appreciation for their concern.

I needed lots of support but could not always bring myself to ask for it or to talk specifically about the cancer. That is understandably hard for others to process and translate into supportive action. I do empathize with not knowing the correct thing to do or say, since I have always regarded myself as a little clumsy in that department. Part of the reason that I wrote and sent my essays to my inner circle was to share what was on my mind and make it easier for them to second-guess my mood.

But through this experience, I can say that, at least for me, there are a few rules of thumb I can offer from my perspective about what not to do and what to do. I will go through them for two reasons. First, I hope if you are tempted to ask these questions, you might think twice. And second, if you are the cancer survivor, don't feel uncomfortable speaking up if you're not okay responding to the probing.

The most obvious rule of thumb is, do not ask about the prognosis. One might think that such an outrageous question is beyond the grasp of any right-thinking individual, but some of the smartest folks I know, even colleagues of mine in the hospital, had the bad judgment to ask me that. My answer ranged from a kindly, "We were lucky to find it early and have every reason to feel hopeful," to a disgusted, "Gee, tick, tock, tick, tock." I think it got around quickly that I did not want to talk about it.

Sometimes, to fill the awkward silence, people asked, "What type of cancer do you have?" I really hated to feel pressure to answer that one, too. After all, I hardly understood it. Outside of the small segment of the medical community who lives and breathes these different diseases are laypeople like me with narrow slices of information gleaned from personal experiences with friends or relatives, pop science on TV, or the Internet. Honestly, most of us are not knowledgeable enough to appreciate the medical nuances involved. The last thing that my band of survivors needs is poorly studied advice, cancer stories whether good or bad, or uninformed assumptions about our life spans and mortality. We are all unique.

I found it very uncomfortable to describe the side effects of the chemotherapy unless it was with my physician or nurse. Nausea, hair loss, weight gain, constant acrid taste in my mouth, infected ports, insomnia combined with overwhelming exhaustion, nose bleeds, diarrhea, and constipation are not physical conditions that can be described delicately. If you are really that curious, perhaps you might consider looking it up online. That said, I did sometimes share what I was experiencing, but I usually did so with a purpose. For one, I couldn't really fake it with my family and close friends. I needed them to give me some space to feel lousy, and second, I needed my colleagues at work to know when to advance and retreat with project responsibilities. Other than that, figure that very few people get through treatment without side effects. They go hand in hand with this lousy disease.

I found it difficult to hear others tell me that I looked terrific when, just that morning, I looked in the mirror and was greeted by a steroid-reddened swollen face from hell. I know you were just looking for something nice to say, but such exaggerations of the truth are pretty transparent and quite unnecessary. We all know that the face of cancer is disturbing. What I found best was encouragement, humor, and honesty. For example, "It's great to see you here at work. You are an inspiration to others facing the disease," or perhaps, "I love your collection of scarves. You have found a way to keep a nice sense of style through your treatment."

The looks from strangers sometimes were worse than words. There is a big difference between empathy and sympathy looks. One shows understanding and support; the other looks like you're on a death watch. I have studied this a little, and I think that the difference is in the eyes. One set is calm, the other an alarmed stare. Sometimes I just hid in my office so that I didn't need to chance seeing those looks.

The trigger to onlookers seems to be my scarf. The scarf is the nonverbal signal that things aren't too swell with me these days. But my husband, God love him, enjoys the perks. He was the first to notice how much more accommodating people are to us in restaurants and when we return retail merchandise. We never seem to have to wait too long for a table, and when we had to make a return recently, the help desk couldn't seem to do enough for us, even though we no longer had the box or receipt the item came with. I keep waiting for my hair to grow another inch so that I can put my scarves away, while he continues to encourage me to wear them. He says that we've never been treated better.

Reflections: One of My Favorite Role Models

I grew up in a large, extended family that I saw frequently. I had many uncles, aunts, and first cousins, all with unique personalities. A few were more traditional in the *Leave It to Beaver* sense, but the rest, like families today, covered the spectrum. What they all had in common was a deep sense of family and a willingness to help each other out in a pinch, all rallying around a shared cause.

The family loyalty is best illustrated on my mother's side, because in the case of the Gelbs, it was organized. Before Medicare and Social Security evolved into entitlements in American life, the Gelbs formed a "Cousins Club," where family needs were discussed and everyone, especially the more prosperous, contributed money to be used as priorities arose. Often, this money was set aside for elderly relatives who typically lived hand to mouth as new immigrants in America at the turn of the twentieth century. The generosity of the Cousins Club also took the form of offering housing for extended family in the close quarters of Brooklyn apartments.

I loved the stories my mother and aunts shared about the manner in which personal issues were discussed. Everyone necessary, mainly the women, crammed into my grandparents' pink-and-black tiled bathroom at the end of the apartment and whispered about diseases, money, loose behavior, and other family gossip. That bathroom was the place to be if you wanted the dirt. As a small child, I sometimes observed groups of women heading into that tiny room together. It took years before I understood the mystery.

My grandparents' apartment was one of the largest of the extended family, with four rooms and a hallway along the side connecting them. It is funny how they didn't count that bathroom as a room in its own right. It was probably the most important place in the whole apartment.

I could see their apartment door when the elevator opened. The elevator had two doors, one solid and one with a folding grate. The air had a distinct smell, neither good nor bad, but one I always associated with our visits. It was only a few steps between the elevator door on the seventh floor and my grandmother's soft embrace. Upon entering from the apartment hallway, the first room was a living room with plastic over the furniture and a candy dish on the coffee table. Years earlier, it had been used as a bedroom to accommodate extra family. Next was a kitchen where blintzes and brisket were cooked practically every time I stayed overnight.

There was also the infamous wooden spoon, a cooking accessory my mother didn't have that was shown to me when my behavior got out of hand. My grandmother would threaten to use it, but being a child unfamiliar with corporal punishment (one of my father's good rules), I didn't understand what Grandma Lily meant when she said, "Do you want me to use this?" I would respond with, "Ok, what are we going to cook today?" Lily, with a quick laugh and careful not to make trouble with my father, would usually see the irony and just giggle, warning me to behave better.

In the center of the apartment was a narrow master bedroom, later used as a den when the children left home. The last bedroom housed all three daughters, sometimes plus some. They shared a little closet and slept together in that small space, despite their nine-year age spread. In one of the more enduring stories many years back, the girls' behavior caused my grandmother to snap. According to my aunts, Grandma chased them around the room, jumping from bed to bed until they all ended up laughing. As children, we loved hearing that story and visualizing my round grandmother jump on the beds, wooden spoon in hand and trying to catch up to three active little girls. It was also where my grandmother later kept her penny jar and ivory mah-jongg set, my favorite toys when I visited.

Between the bedrooms was the famous bathroom. Other relatives lived in the building and frequently stopped by to visit. There always was the buzz of family. In the hustle and bustle, our names became

Jane-ala and Ann-ala, the affectionate Yiddish variations reserved for childhood.

The apartment had a history of its own, with family losses including my mother's little brother, Howard, who died of blood poisoning during the era before antibiotics, and her grandfather, who died there while she was alone with him, a girl only in her early teens. The apartment also had a strong history of happiness and sharing. My mother's cousins, Joanne and Helene, lived with them for several years. Their father, my great-uncle Jack, had bad luck picking healthy wives, the first two dying far too young and each leaving him a daughter. While he was getting his life back in order, Grandma Lily would scoop up her nieces and add them to her brood. Through this, the girls of that generation became very close and shared lots of their own secrets. Secrets were really big back then. Bit by bit, they are starting to come out when we get together. I think that my generation's openness must be coaxing our mothers to share more.

My grandparents worked with their hands. As I am told, Grandpa Leo delivered soap to Chinese cleaners and owned a car, a rare possession for city dwellers. The car was reputed to always have a gritty back seat. My grandmother, Lillian, who completed up to eighth grade, was a milliner and clever with designing and constructing hats, a fashion that was in vogue at the time and extended well beyond the Orthodox Jewish community. The women at home wore housecoats, loose dresses made of cotton that were the casual wear of their day. I suppose they were a lot like sweatsuits are for us now. She was also a marvelous knitter. When Lily died, her sister, Bea, asked only for Lily's knitting needles. My heart skips a beat every time I think of the sentimentality of her gesture. The sisters must have spent many hours knitting and talking while helping each other through their life challenges.

Grandma Lily's parents, Jenny and Adolf, had a bed-and-breakfast type of establishment long before that term was in fashion. It was in the country at Hunter Mountain, just north of New York City, years before ski resorts were built. The kids would spend time helping them in the summer, often setting up the pins in the old fashioned, manual bowling alleys. My great-grandmother Jenny, not trusting adolescent boys (especially my father), would see that there was always an escort on any hikes up the mountain.

They all worked very hard. Even family outings were hard work, especially for Lily. A typical summer Sunday trip consisted of a day at Riis Park, a beach in the Rockaways, near what was, at that time, an airport called Floyd Bennett Field. Lily would get up early and make tons of egg salad and tuna sandwiches for lunch. Leo prepared thermoses full of orange drinks, and they would pack the car full of heavy, wooden beach chairs, an umbrella, and blankets, and then head for the beach. My grandfather reportedly had a knack for scheduling each leg of the trip at the height of traffic, years before automobile air conditioning was invented. Once everything was arranged on the sand, hunger set in and everything Lily had prepared vanished, and then they all swam and played beach games. Before they knew it, the process kicked into reverse, again facing traffic in the heat of the day and all vying to be the first to hop into the little pink-and-black tiled bathroom to wash off the irritating sand trapped in their swim suits. Of course, Lily showered last, with the satisfaction she had provided a good day for her family.

My mother's youngest sibling was Connie, who was only eighteen years old when I was born. She became a frequent babysitter and joined her parents for the weekly trek out from Brooklyn to New Jersey on Sundays. Ann and I were the first grandchildren and the lucky recipients of endless family attention.

Connie was particularly close to her parents since she was the last to leave home to marry. Many comparisons were made between Connie and her mother Lily. Both thrived on the energy of people in their lives. Connie was always lots of fun and had an infectious laugh, somewhat like her mother's. Perhaps it was being the youngest of her siblings, or more likely her innate personality, but she loved people.

Connie was fawned over by the adults, siblings, and cousins. She was an adorable little girl with a head of blonde, curly hair. She was only five years old when my parents started dating, and my father took her on like a little sister. In return, she was the goldmine of family information, loving everyone and judging no one. Over the years, we were very close. She became, to no one's surprise, a kindergarten teacher, the absolute favorite in her school district.

Connie had an open door for her friends and family, somehow making each of us feel like her favorite. She wasn't interested in the superficial unless it involved a great new recipe, and immediately dove into the deeper issues, empathizing with our dilemmas, giving advice when asked, and always, always following up later with phone calls to see how things were going. She checked on me frequently during my divorced years and first bout with breast cancer, contributing positive thoughts, generously offering her beach house for short reprieves, and rooting me on. There was simply no way to give back as much as she gave.

A few years ago, she was diagnosed with cancer and passed away last year. She fought courageously for several years and always adapted graciously to her gradually reducing capabilities. Her many friends and family members went to her funeral to honor her. She had asked that the women carry her casket, as her connections to her girl friends were so very strong. There was no shortage of volunteers.

Connie taught me many valuable lessons, but with respect to illness, she showed me through her behavior just how important support from family and friends can be. She never lost her sense of hope and always absorbed the hard punches that come with cancer without losing herself in the process. Strangely, she still feels alive in my mind. Although I miss her terribly, I can still very easily conjure up her face and hear her laugh. It always makes me smile. It is the kind of smile that comes with deep, warm memories.

The Gelb girls: Connie, Gilda, Bobbie

Lillian and Leo Gelb, my maternal grandparents

How I Met My Husband

The biggest downside to having married at nineteen was that I was never single as a young adult. I had no real dating experience, and after six fun years of traveling and finishing school with D, I quickly became a young parent of three. I seemed programmed for marriage and family life, but suddenly in my early thirties, my marriage ended and I found myself excruciatingly unprepared for the mating dance ahead. When I was thirty-three, most of my male counterparts hadn't married yet, didn't have children, or were far earlier in their careers than my ex-husband. It was near impossible to start on any kind of even ground. I found it impossible to look with interest at men much older than I, even though they were far better matches for me in the more important areas of life such as children and maturity.

I was so impressionable and inexperienced that I can't help but shake my head now at the crazy dating episodes I encountered. I once ate at Bennigan's with three different blind dates on the same day—twice at the same table with the same waiter. None made it to a second date, but I can't help wondering if the waiter thought I was a "working girl." He looked at me very strangely when I walked in that evening with a new, third man.

I don't even remember how many Barrys, Roberts, or Mikes I dated anymore. After some time, I lost count. On one date, I ate at a seedy Italian joint with a Jewish blind date who organized traveling carnivals. Trying to impress me, he pulled out a gigantic wad of bills, tipping me off that he was in the cash business. He looked me up and down, and then said in a sultry Brando voice, "You would look delicious in a mink." Clearly, he hadn't looked too closely. I think I might have been wearing my warm argyle socks and cotton underwear on that chilly winter night, hardly the costume of anticipation. Later at the door when I said good-bye, he asked if I would see him again. I told him that I didn't think things had much potential between us, to which he replied, "Well, can we at least fool around?" That night I locked the doors tightly behind me and slept with one eye open.

Too many married men took a shot. What were they thinking? No way would I have ever become the other woman. I had no intention of either breaking up someone else's family or playing second fiddle. On a friend's advice, I gave them a quarter and suggested they call me if ever single. Little by little, I became jaded.

I did have a lot of fun too, but I repeatedly made the mistake of allowing the wrong relationships to advance. The hard lesson for me was that I tended to get attached, even if the relationship wasn't good for a lifetime. That led to some difficult breakups for me and the children. One in particular involved a man a couple of years younger than I. Although lots of fun when the mood was right, he had a deplorable track record with women, even keeping a score book on how many times he slept with them. That discovery came near the end of the relationship. I wasn't totally out of my mind. But what I did learn from that long on-and-off romance was the importance of having fun, letting go, and trying new things.

As I entered my mid-forties, I had an epiphany. I was only dating from there on out. No more exclusive relationships unless I saw serious prospects for a future. Eureka! It took close to twelve years to get that simple lesson into my head!

Shortly after, I put a profile on a Jewish Internet dating site and met my husband. I had just turned forty-five, and some of my girlfriends had planned a birthday brunch in my honor. I had been given a few lewd birthday cards and a photo was taken of me holding one of them while wearing quite a large smile on my face. I cropped my face shot to use for the profile and must have tuned into a high male libido frequency, as measured by the flood of e-mail responses. Being a novice with the Internet, I laughed and enjoyed the e-mails, moving from one to the next, always figuring that they would be automatically saved. Instead, they were all deleted. I shrugged it off and figured that the entertainment was enough of a reward. A few days later, I received a second e-mail from one guy, now my husband, asking why he hadn't made the cut. I remembered his first response, now in the recycling bin. Something felt familiar about him, something smart, self-effacing, and non-frantic. I knew by his name that I hadn't dated him before, because David, the name of my ex, was one name that I absolutely would have remembered.

It was my nature to size people up face-to-face and not waste time flirting online. So we met within a couple of weeks. As for the height, on a good day, David barefoot is about one inch taller than I—so we really did have a chance to meet eye to eye. He asked me to select a romantic restaurant for our first meeting. I didn't know if this was a line or if he was really serious, so I told him that anywhere I eat is romantic and picked a place right off the interstate exit in case things didn't go well. When I walked in, I saw him standing by the bar and immediately had a great vibe. I just had that comfortable, first-impression click. Later that night alone in my home, I realized that the dinner, even at that ordinary restaurant, was the best I had had in many years.

Very soon afterwards, I switched my heels for flats, and the rest is history. I must have spent a fortune on shoes during those dating years. At five feet, eight inches, I was more often than not the wrong height for my dates. It seemed like I was always buying shoes.

My plan for a European bike trip morphed into a romantic vacation in London and Paris. David convinced me that it would be far more fun and safer than a bike trip with strangers. He was then, as he usually is now, completely correct. For nostalgia, we sometimes go back to that restaurant near the highway and reminisce about our first date. The food is lousy, but the dinners are always wonderful.

As I look back, I am certain that I sensed his empathetic qualities. David's natural ability to bring positive energy to difficult situations has helped me through many scary health moments. And his belief in the cumulative power of reason, continual advances in health care, and love has helped keep my sense of hope alive every day.

When I Need a Quick Chuckle

A few years back when Carrie, my eldest, was on the cusp of adolescence and her younger sister Laura was finishing grade school, we had a morning episode of *Our Family's Funniest Moments.*

Carrie, always a calm, people-centered child, was starting to face a different chapter in her life. Her newly active hormones were surging, and that morning in particular she was storming around the house angry and snapping over minor infractions. As any parent of a young adolescent girl knows, it is at times like these that you breathe deeply, get them out the door to the bus, and pray that they return at the end of the school day in a better mood.

Laura, who had been struggling for a while with awful stomachaches, had worked very hard the previous day to obtain a stool sample for lab testing. The collection of this sample was traumatic. Laura required complete privacy, was totally grossed out, and swore that she'd rather die than to ever be subjected to such indignity again. Once collected, the sample was stored in a brown paper bag and placed inside the door of the refrigerator.

Breakfast finished, Carrie grabbed her book bag, stopped at the refrigerator for her lunch, and headed out the front door without a kiss or her usual sweet, "Bye, Mom, have a nice day." Laura and Ben's bus wasn't due for a half hour, so they continued to relax at the table, mildly amused by their big sister's performance.

Suddenly, a wave of panic passed through me, and before I could think, I opened the refrigerator door to look inside at the remaining lunch bags. I counted three with lunches and none with a stool sample. Carrie had already walked half way down the block, and I was in my flannel nightgown. For a few seconds, I pondered the poetic justice of Carrie opening her yummy lunch bag at school. A psychotic laugh escaped from deep within, but in spite of the thought, I headed for the door. Fortunately, my good instincts as a parent overrode my sardonic desire for justice.

Half way down the street, I caught up with Carrie. She looked at me in my nightwear with an expression of total embarrassment. Pretending I wasn't really there, she kept walking. I yelled, "Carrie, give me your lunch. Trust me, you don't want that one." Stopping for a moment, she took a peek, screamed, and switched bags. An enormous laugh of relief exploded from both of us, and we quickly headed in opposite directions.

I still chastise myself for even having a moment of indecision. It came down to the thought of putting Laura through the trauma of another specimen collection. But it did leave the four of us with one of our finest and funniest family tales and is always good for chuckle when needed.

It's Time to Begin Chemotherapy, Again

My breast cancer chemotherapy treatment was close to a decade ago. By the time I finished, I was filled with a complicated mix of emotions. On the one hand, my veins and stamina were a mess, and that part of me was screaming out for relief. On the other hand, I knew that it would be a free fall from that point on. I had a type of breast cancer that did not respond to drugs like Tamoxifen and similar others that came later. I needed to hope that the chemo I had received destroyed any microscopic disease traveling through my system. Apparently it did. So far, ten years later, I seem to be cured of breast cancer.

This time around, I take a deep breath and hope this more toxic cocktail will do the same for my ovarian/peritoneal cancer. The stakes are higher with fewer options. The deep cleansing breaths I learned close to thirty years ago in Lamaze classes are helpful as I try not to look down. I know that medicine has not come as far with this disease as it has with breast cancer, but I am in a corner and have to trust that the chemotherapy will do its job.

The evening before my first treatment, my husband and I treated ourselves to a forbidden vice: ice cream sundaes at Dairy Queen. That deliciously smooth vanilla ice cream covered with warm caramel sauce and toasted pecans just makes me pant. Not once did I think about the calories, the next day's plan, or anything else. All I could absorb was the orgasmic delight of those wonderful flavors in my mouth. We ate in total quiet, not allowing anything to interfere with our concentration. Those wonderful sensations were just so indescribable.

Earlier that day, we reminisced about my/our first chemotherapy appointment. It was an autumn day soon after my lumpectomy, and I was very nervous. Upon arriving at the infusion suite, I was assigned a chair. David and I looked at each other and smiled. The room looked like a hair salon. The only differences were the IV poles and optional drapes between the chairs. I sat in a seat by a beautiful set of windows and a door heading out to a sunny patio. A few minutes later, a wildly nervous man came running by us heading straight to the door. He was wearing a hospital gown with the back open, dragging his IV pole, and holding a cigarette. My jaw dropped. He was totally overcome with the need for a smoke. A couple of nurses were chasing after him, trying to calm him down and bring him back inside. Finally, looking at each other, they decided to let the man have his cigarette outdoors, shaking their heads sadly all the while. His wife, totally fed up, and most likely on her last nerve, announced, "I have spoken to hospice, and they simply won't take him yet." Sadly, she wasn't even joking. By that point, she was a caretaker totally out of energy. David and I looked at each other and began to laugh. This was material for movies, and we knew that it couldn't possibly be an ordinary occurrence. We were right. From that point on, all was smooth sailing with patients making light conversation and offering encouragement and treats galore.

The story still brings a smile to my face as I think about what this time will bring. I am now equipped with internal IV ports, so all of that poking will be avoided, and I will be able to enjoy the summer with my sleeveless tops and non-bruised arms. I am bringing a terrific book that I downloaded on a Kindle, a gift from my wonderful book club friends. I am also bringing an iPod with spa music in case the medicine makes me sleepy. I feel prepared and am determined to take my best shot at treatment. After all, I have everything to live for.

So, what actually did happen? Not what I expected at all. I turned out to have a strong allergic reaction to the Taxol® I had taken, or at least the coating that they put around the microscopic beads. Even with the steroid pills taken to avoid such a reaction, it took just one cc of this drug to set my body into a tailspin requiring an emergency response. Thank goodness the nurses and my doctor were at my side with an immediate change in treatment course. Looking back, the reaction lasted only a few minutes. It was the longest I ever held my breath! It felt like an out-of-body experience as I watched everyone scurry around and I felt my body cramp. Fortunately, they were able to replace the Taxol® with a new drug containing a less toxic coating.

It is a lot more expensive, but whoever said that I was a cheap date! In the end, it all worked out, and the way the staff kept their cool helped keep me from panicking.

David was a little freaked and cancelled his night meeting; an unheard-of move! The extra attention everyone gave me was kind of nice, and I got back to my Kindle story, *People of the Book*. They tell me that my hair will begin to fall out three weeks from now. I think I will get my buzz cut before our trip to the Outer Banks. Strangely, I have chosen not to dwell on that part. I keep trying to focus on the bigger picture: killing the evil cells. At times like these, one just shakes it off and focuses on making it through to the next minute.

The Lows and the Highs

Two months after my surgery and a few days after my first round of chemotherapy, I hit my nadir. That's what the doctors call the low point of each chemotherapy cycle. Three days after my treatment, I was expecting to feel like I was on the upswing and instead felt like I was coming down with flu. My whole body was hurting, the nausea was constant, and to top it off, my head was aching as my hair follicles began to throw in the towel and break down. In spite of my short haircut, I felt and looked like a golden retriever shedding for the summer. In short, I was miserable. I was tired of keeping up a strong front for everyone around me and spent the day feeling sorry for myself. We planned to leave for our vacation in the Outer Banks the next day, and I was worried I wouldn't feel well enough to have a good time. I had also committed to going back to work in two weeks and was beginning to think I had been overly optimistic in making that decision.

I pushed through the day with the help of my daughter, Laura, who drove me around to finish last minute errands, and David, who packed up the car and quietly let me moan and groan, nodding his head from time to time with a look of empathy. At 9:00 PM, I took a pill and fell into a deep, withdrawn sleep.

Five in the morning came in no time, and we were up and on our way. The Outer Banks of North Carolina are over 450 miles from our home, and our blended family was driving down in four cars. Everyone had planned to leave early in the morning to get a jump on the traffic. Fortunately, I was beginning to feel a bit better. Although I did not tempt fate by trying to read or knit in the car, the ride down was relaxing in spite of its length. For the first day that week, I did not need to take any nausea medication.

Upon arriving, we all showered and headed to the sand dunes for a family photo shoot with a professional photographer. It must sound crazy, but I didn't want to make my treatment the focus of our trip. Last year, our photos on the beach were terrific but a painful effort. We must have taken 150 photos in an attempt to take one great one of all of the kids. This year I decided we were due for a treat and hired a pro. After a half hour of laughter and posing, I knew that the decision was a good one. Back at the house, we had a dinner of Southern barbeque (my favorite food these days since barbeque sauce works great on cutting through the metallic taste in my mouth) and headed to bed early.

The following day was magical. I woke up feeling terrific. By 11:00 AM, I was sitting under the beach umbrella watching my family play in the water and laugh with each other. I looked at Laura holding the football and recalled her standing before me more than twenty years ago laughing with pleasure as she held a toy pony in each hand. I thought about how timeless the beach could make me feel. I glanced over at Ben as he teased his girlfriend, and I recalled the huge sand castles that my Aunt Bobbie made with him when he was a toddler. She had worked with Ben for over an hour on that architectural wonder, and once done, he snuck his little toes mischievously into its foundation until it fell apart. Glancing over at Carrie, ripe in her pregnancy, I saw her contouring a hole in the sand to fit snugly around her growing belly. She was missing the feeling of sleeping on her stomach. I smiled at the memory of her in the sandbox. She never tired of all of the creative options that sat waiting for her in the sand.

David and my two stepsons, Jordan and Max, made their way to the beach and jumped right into the activity. Even though our five children don't see each other all together often, they seem to meld instantly. All morning, they swam, threw balls, read, and talked. I started feeling higher than a kite. Behind my sunglasses, I began to feel confident that everything would be okay.

The Outer Banks, 2007

The Quail

"So I lost him. But I shall always see
In my mind
The warm, yellow sun, and the ether free;
The vista's sky, and the white cloud trailing,
Trailing behind,—
And below the young earth's summer-green arbors,
And on high the eagle, —sailing, sailing
Into far skies and unknown harbors"
—*The Eagle*, E. E. Cummings

When my brother Leo was around six years old, we had a neighbor up the street who kept a pet quail in his house. One day, as a prank, Leo and his friend Peter opened the front door of the neighbor's house, letting the quail escape. I can't imagine why they were opening front doors of other people's homes. Neither boy was terribly mischievous on his own, but together they always seemed to stir up trouble. Who could possibly understand what was on the minds of a couple of six-year-old boys? A few months earlier, they let the air out of all of the red Schwinn bikes on the rack at the elementary school. Since most everyone walked or cycled to school, this caused a huge problem. Why they left the blue, black, and yellow bikes untouched remains a mystery.

We didn't know these neighbors all that well. This house always seemed to have lots of turnover, and to the best of my recollection, no one lived there for more than a few years at a clip. The children on the block found the place a bit spooky. A tall man with glasses (weren't all adults tall back then?) who never seemed to smile at anyone now lived there with his wife. I don't think they had children of their own, and we rarely saw them outdoors. I no longer remember their names. But that day in particular, the curious nature of little boys got the best of Leo and Peter. They couldn't resist opening the front door when the couple was not home. Back in those days, about fifty years ago, no one bothered locking their home during the daytime unless they were on vacation.

Later that afternoon, the tall man with glasses showed up at our house hopping mad. Pop was home and greeted the man and welcomed him in for a drink. Knowing Pop, he probably saw this as a great opportunity to move up cocktail hour by a few hours. Instead, the man began yelling at my father about his delinquent son, the precious nature of the bird, and the emotional trauma this incident had caused his wife and him. My father called Leo downstairs (he was hiding in his room) and had him admit to the crime and apologize. Pop also offered the guy some money so he could buy a new bird. The peace offerings were angrily refused.

Pop, already suspicious of a grown man who valued birds more than an apology from a six-year-old kid, and at that point having no idea what this man was after, began to laugh. He thought it was some kind of a joke. You see, Pop and a few of his friends on the block were known for their own pranks; like the time my father and Bob Aaron next door rigged Dave Favin's garage door so that up was down and down was up. Bob and Dave were both highly trained scientists in their professional lives, but around the neighborhood, they and my father were always playing tricks on each other. It was the first electric garage door on the block and their good natured target, Dave, went crazy trying to figure out what was wrong. Afterwards, they had a good laugh and drank together.

But back to "Quailgate." My father's temper was starting to rise after the neighbor insisted that Pop hunt down the bird and bring it home alive. The image of Pop, upon an order from the man with glasses, crawling around in the shrubs trying to catch a bird was so outrageous that it even makes me laugh thinking about it today. This guy had no idea who he was dealing with.

By that point, with all of us holding back laughter, Pop asked the poor man to leave. My mother, a bit embarrassed and worried about making enemies with the neighbors, made Leo write an apology letter, while my father joked about the whole thing for years. Lucky for Leo, he never got punished.

I never quite understood why anyone would want to keep a quail for a pet. To the best of my knowledge, quails are not great house birds, certainly not rare, but a breed that fights for space when confined, hides when feeling threatened, and treasures its freedom—quite like me.

My Name, Just Two Four-Letter Words

The name on my birth certificate is Jane Loeb, just two simple four-letter words. My parents loved simplicity and saw no reason for a middle name or a longer, more common 1950s name like Susan or Patricia. I was almost Jenny, named after my great-grandmother, but short English names sounded pleasant to my folks, so my sister was named Ann, and then when I came along, Jane ruled the day.

When I got married at age nineteen, I changed my name to Jane Loeb Taylor, where it stayed put for twenty-eight years. At the time of that marriage, my very little identification was updated, and after the divorce, I left my name unchanged to preserve a sense of family unity with my Taylor children. In the meantime, it had also become my known professional identity.

Nine years ago, when I remarried, I became Jane Loeb Taylor Rubin. For the sake of thoroughness, I chose to incorporate all of my collective identities. I did not want to sacrifice any important chapters in my life. By this point, I probably had most of the school girls of my youth beat, barring the Catholic girls with their christening names added in.

Always slow on paperwork, all I had to prove this lengthy new identity was my marriage certificate. I felt no rush to update my passport, social security number, or driver's license. Needless to say, none of my credit cards were changed either. One month after our wedding, 9/11 occurred, and air travel was never the same.

My husband's family tradition was to pack up the children around the Christmas/New Year's holiday and head to Florida to visit his elderly parents. Now with a new family, we made an effort to bring along my children to get acquainted with his family. One particular trip, we were only traveling with the three boys. What we did not know was that David's travel agent, in an effort to be one step ahead, booked my ticket in my newly married name.

The morning of our flight, we headed to the airport in the freezing dawn and stood for close to an hour on an endless outdoor check-in line at Newark Airport. Finally at the front, we were told to our surprise and dismay that my identification was not sufficient. I was sent inside to rebook my flight under my prior three names. Meanwhile, with time tight, I sent the boys on their way and assured them that we would catch up in Florida.

As it turned out, their flight was overbooked, and they were bumped because they were so late checking in. The attendant rebooked their group on the only other flight that day to Florida. Unfortunately, it was scheduled to land on the other side of the state. Continental graciously provided a minibus to transport the displaced travelers to their original destination on the east coast. Their ride was an adventure in its own right. My tired husband amused himself with the antics of three wired adolescent boys, and they eventually found their way to our motel. In the meantime, I was put in a single seat on a different plane and arrived hours ahead of them. I took a cab to our motel that turned out not at all similar to the luxury resort we shopped for online. The marquee out front announced that Diamond Dave was performing in the lounge for our entertainment that evening. I was already counting down the hours until we headed back home.

Ever since I added my fourth name, all of my medical records have been a mess. The pharmacy attendant always has trouble finding my prescriptions because the name choice on the bottle is like musical chairs. I even announced at my farewell party from my last job five years back, that the real reason I was taking a new job was to finally change my name once and for all. For years, old work acquaintances still called me at my current job asking for Jane Taylor, someone who no longer existed ... or at least was not in the operator's directory.

So, aside from the empathy I feel for every woman faced with multiple name changes, I ask myself why I changed it in the first or second place. Why didn't I just go back to the simple name with which I began? At the time, it came down to the negative symbolism of living with two four-letter words. Now, I have to laugh at the irony and fuss, because there are two four-letter words that come to mind when I think about my cancer dilemma, and they certainly aren't Jane Loeb.

WWJD

At the risk of sounding overconfident, I will admit that finally, at this point of my life, I usually make the right decision. I am probably right over 80 percent of the time, possibly closing in on 90 percent. But that type of batting average didn't even begin to happen until I turned forty.

"WWJD" ("What Would Jane Do") was first coined by one of my daughter's work friends. He was a subordinate in a hospital emergency department I supervised for several years. I had earned a reputation there as a strong decision maker, particularly when on the spot decisions were called for. In emergency medicine, success only requires a few skills: good common sense, the ability to collect facts fast, a focus on the patient and family's needs, the willingness to take some risk in the interest of moving the process along, and not missing a "golden window" of care. Most of these skills were acquired at home while I ran my little household on my own. We all knew that his cleverness was just a thinly disguised flirtation with my daughter. But in spite of that, the phrase quickly caught on at home, and to this day, a decade later, I still sometimes hear it in a teasing tone.

As a youngster, I loved to be in charge, and for a time in the beginning part of my life, it seemed like nothing could go wrong. I was a confident child, became the head of the student council in high school, went to a great college, married my high school sweetheart, had beautiful children, and so forth. But some of this was a mirage, because I couldn't see that the foundation was slowly crumbling. Looking back, I now understand that during my twenties and thirties I made some rather key mistakes.

I discovered years back that there is a fine line between a healthy level of confidence and being overconfident and arrogant. For me, the latter were two mortal demons I have worked hard to part with. Over my life, I have learned that my mistakes have offered valuable learning opportunities, and that humility is at times a painful gateway to understanding. This late-in-life ability to step back, swallow my pride, and see things from a different point of view has been the fastest learning tool I have discovered.

One notable mistake I made was with my first husband. At age twenty-four, we thought we knew it all. We packed up for a month in Europe with new backpacks, maps, and guidebooks. We had planned a $20/day vacation complete with a rental car, camping equipment, and guidebook of pensions. Most of our plans were figured out on the road. This vagabond vacation was, for the most part, lots of fun, and the lack of structure led to many spontaneous experiences and discoveries. But in our arrogance, we made a key error when it came to Greece.

Halfway through the vacation, we boarded a plane at 11:00 PM in Rome heading for Athens, Greece. It was scheduled to arrive at 1:00 AM. Looking back thirty years later, I cannot recall why we chose such a late flight, but knowing us, it must have had something to do with not losing a sightseeing day in Rome.

D had an amazing visual memory. During the flight, while I tried to catch a nap, he studied the street map of Athens, selecting a few alternative pensions in the downtown. Upon landing, we headed directly into the city to find them. What neither of us had factored in was that our maps were in English, and all of the actual street signs were in Greek. Within an hour of our landing, we were totally lost and found ourselves down by the docks with the sailors and rough creatures of the late night. In our exhaustion, we picked a place to sleep and headed inside. As we climbed the stairs, we passed numerous couples in heated embraces. Something in the air was pretty fishy. A painted woman showed us to our room. Once there, we realized that the door was barely on the hinges, and the lock was gone. While I focused on sleep, my husband realized that we had checked into a brothel. He insisted that we leave, so I collected my belongings. We stepped into the hallway, and I engaged the madam, who stood surrounded by several thugs, in a negotiation for our, yes, three dollars back. Instead of looking at me, I noticed that they were glaring at my husband.

Realizing that they were not negotiating with me at all, I politely settled for one dollar and left feeling relieved. I will admit that I have never been particularly good natured when I'm overtired, but I surely didn't want to see D beaten up.

Years later, I recollect numerous examples of a less dramatic nature, all following the same pattern. I made assumptions without checking the facts and proceeded to find myself in the middle of difficult situations. It really took until my divorce and many hours of therapy to let down my well-armored guard and appreciate the importance of self reflection and reality checks. This did lead to some slow changes in my outlook on others, me, and my workplace. Like a new deer on shaky legs, I practiced better listening skills, worked on empathy, and learned how to acknowledge others' ideas. Change came slowly, and one way I practiced was with my children.

Knowing how hard this understanding came to me, I tried to stage mistakes for them so that they could practice getting back on track. Since we were typically a band of four, I needed them to help with maps while driving and, for fun, put them in charge of reading subway maps in other cities. Although there were some occasions when I preferred not to be lost, my mantra was "It's okay to get lost," knowing that we could always figure out a way to get back on course. When the kids got their driver's permits, I took each of them driving in the snow to practice driving on slippery roads. Some of my boyfriends through this period thought I was nuts for staging mistakes, but I wanted the children to know that if they ever got in a jam, they could think on their feet and not panic. I can honestly say now that they all have pretty good street smarts and keep a level head under pressure.

But one thing I do notice is that the kids really hate it that I am right so often. I have to try very hard to keep my thoughts quiet, not offer unsolicited advice, give them space to figure things out for themselves, and hope that they have the right tools. Since I know that most of my growth came from making my own mistakes, I know that I need to let them figure things out for themselves too. The temptation to talk is sometimes overwhelming, but I try really hard to simply listen. I am, however, considering a subliminal winking system. One wink for right and two for wrong. I wonder how long it will take for them to catch on.

All in a Name

The Jews have a tradition of naming new babies after the deceased. As I understand it, the rationale behind this tradition is that by selecting a name from a family member who has passed, the memory of his/her life will be memorialized. The idea is thoughtful in a way, but like most traditions people dutifully follow, this naming tradition often leaves me feeling more empty than full.

For example, most people I know who have embraced this practice have done so half-heartedly. Often they have not known the family member well or loved the name. So out of some degree of observance, or to please others in the family, the name is morphed into either a middle position or is sometimes the first letter attached to a new string of letters more pleasing to the parents. That might be okay, except for the memorializing part. I wonder how much the child ever really learns about the person who had that name last. Are great stories, contributions, or physical qualities ever shared? Who was the person that filled up that name and life?

My sister and I were not named after anyone. There were no stories and accomplishments to remember through our names and no old jokes or laughs to pass along. We were given names that pleased our parents' ears and left to carve out our own unique identities. My brother, on the other hand, was named in 1957 after our grandfather, who had recently passed away when my mother was only three months pregnant.

There was great controversy surrounding the use of Grandpa's name, Leopold, an old European name. My father, predictably strong in his convictions, felt that Grandpa's name should be used in full or not at all. My mother was torn. With the names Leopold and Loeb still then associated in the public's mind with convicted murderers, she was wary of naming her son Leopold Loeb. She was concerned that a name connected to badness would be a burden for him to carry through his life. Her grandfather's name was Adolph, and because of the Holocaust, no Jew ever used his name again. After many lengthy discussions, my folks settled on Leo Paul Loeb. My mother really loved the name Paul and tried to convince Pop to agree to Paul Leo, but in the end, my father felt he had compromised enough by breaking the name into two and creating a middle name.

It seemed like there was so much emotion connected with Leo's birth. Since my mother had been pregnant when her dad died, there was still great sadness in our home. Her father had adored her, and she was missing him terribly. That loss in itself would have been plenty, but there was more to the story.

When my mother was a small child, her younger brother, Howard, was injured and later died of sepsis. It was before antibiotics, and tragedies like this with three-year-old children were all too common. In some way, she felt responsible for the event, and it was very important to her to bring a boy into the world. Having her father gone before he could meet her first son added another layer of loss. Needless to say, using her father's name held high importance to her. In a way, it layered the past onto the present and helped fasten together the players in our family's circle of life and death. Perhaps using his name helped her grieve as she bonded with her new son.

Leo's life was always enriched with stories of his grandfather, who was a hardworking, family-centered, dutiful man. Interestingly, my brother Leo had many of those same qualities. I wonder, though, how many came from his personal wiring, and how many resulted from the stories. If they were learned, did they stymie his sense of exploration and creativity, qualities for which Leopold or Leo were never known? I suppose it will remain a mystery. In the end, it may just be a case of taking the good with the bad.

I thought about names a lot when I was pregnant, and in the end I selected names like mine that were not attached to anyone. I had lost some elderly relatives in the years immediately preceding parenthood, and the names Helen and Abby were up for grabs. Both names sounded old to me, and I couldn't imagine giving them to a baby. I assumed that a name that started off with "Hell" was a recipe for disaster. Since

I hadn't been terribly close to either relative, I decided to pick names that I liked.

We moved from Ann Arbor to St. Louis when I was pregnant with Carrie. The attorney who helped us with our house closing also represented the estate of two St. Louis sisters who never married and had both recently passed away. In their will, they agreed to pay the first Jewish family in the city one thousand dollars if they named their newborn child Ida Rose or Rose Ida, their two first names. My father thought we were crazy not to do it, but I could not, even though the money seemed like a fortune to us. I was much younger then and had not thought through the real meaning of using someone's name or why strangers would want their names memorialized through people they did not know.

Back then, I also did not fully understand why my mother had felt so deeply about her father's name. I now understand that it was a way of keeping strong, heartfelt memories alive every day. I find myself wondering about my father's name, Robert, my brother's name, Leo, and my Aunt Connie's names, and if anyone will choose to use them. What about mine? Will it be the letter J or the whole enchilada? Will it come with good stories or spotlight my foibles? Will there be unfair expectations, or will it be a jinx? Is it worth doing such a thing to an innocent child?

Now that I have had time to think about it more, I really like that my mother's reason for naming my brother after her dad was not out of duty or observance. She chose the name out of a deep feeling of love, the very warmest way to welcome a new life into the world.

"Mom, How Does It Really Feel?"

Carrie suggested I write more about my emotional experience with cancer. I was left wondering if my writing was simply scratching the surface, or if my stories were disguising a deeper set of feelings. So this morning, I challenged myself to dig a bit deeper and come face to face with the written reflections of my feelings.

When I was a child, I would feel badly for other people who had problems but believed that those bad things could not happen to me. I thought that I had some magical protective coating that would keep me from illness. Aging, sickness, and misfortune were for others. When I lost my front teeth, somehow I just adapted and stopped thinking about it as a defect. Even as a worker in the health-care industry, I separated myself from other peoples' sad realities with a self-made emotional buffer. The first time I had cancer, I spent a lot of time in denial. Having cancer again has made me think more about my lifecycle and the cycle size I have seemed to inherit. I know that most of that is out of our hands. Because in the end, nature rules. None of us is given a guarantee of immortality. I don't really spend much time thinking, "Why me?" If anything, I think, "Why not me?"

So, after the intellectualizing, how do I really feel deep inside?

I am disappointed and very sad that this illness is happening to me now. I am in the harvest season of my life. My family, career, and interests have matured into the life of which I always dreamed. I worked so hard to climb to this place and don't want to be cheated out of the view. I want to know my grandchildren firsthand instead of existing as a piece of fiction told through others' stories. I want tangible relationships full of emotion as I watch them grow.

I want to be around for my children as they navigate through their adult years. I have a unique and deep love for each of them. The idea of not being here as they marry and become parents is too sad to bear. I want to support them when they are faced with tough decisions, help them face their disappointments, and celebrate their successes. I don't want to be just in their hearts. I want to be available in the most palpable sense of the word. I want to know them as adults.

I want to grow old with my husband. I spent a lifetime searching for a man I could connect with on so many levels. We have had a great marriage and friendship for the last ten years, and I want it to continue on for many more. I want to share many more dreams together, become doting grandparents, and travel to new places. I certainly don't want to go out in midlife as a needy, sickly wife. I want to be there to give back to him, too.

I hate having to endure chemo *again*. I know that I am not feeling the cancer now. Actually, I don't even know what it feels like to have cancer. Ironically, both times the cancer was caught so early that I never had symptoms. What I have now are the feelings associated with the treatment, but it really sucks. It sucks to have two ports, lose my hair, feel queasy, a constant metallic taste in my mouth, and run out of energy before I have accomplished much during the day. I told my surgeon that the best I felt for the last several months was the day before my surgery. It has been a tough ride since.

I remember Pop once saying that we come into the world alone and later leave it alone. I didn't pay much attention at the time, but I also never forgot it. Now, as I fight this disease, I know what he meant. Even with my extraordinary family and friends, it is terribly lonely to be sick.

But strangely, something inside me is protecting me from depression and despair. I must have come wired with strong defense mechanisms, because I keep moving forward, slow and steady. I have a deep belief that this treatment will be worth the struggle. In the least, it will give me a jumpstart on fighting this awful disease. I have hope.

Tennis Lessons

Ben, my youngest, was a bundle of kinetic energy from the moment he could walk. He was the textbook case of a little boy too busy on his sturdy legs to learn to speak, sit still, or stay out of mischief. Following two sisters and growing up in an all-female household, the stage was set for a little boy who seemed to be constantly getting into some type of trouble.

For us, the safety valve was sports. Once Ben turned five, I enrolled him in the town's recreational sports programs. He played soccer, basketball, and baseball. Ben was clearly a natural athlete, and with little encouragement, he devoted every last ounce of enthusiasm into the game at hand. These physical outlets helped him channel energy in a positive direction and also taught him many important lessons. Unfortunately, with these particular sports, one of earliest lessons was if your dad coached, you had a place on the team and sometimes even a key position in the game. My hours of field-side rooting weren't enough to offset the "dad factor." To some degree, Ben was able to overcome this obstacle by excelling to a point where he clearly deserved important positions. It also didn't hurt that his enthusiasm and competitive spirit helped engage his teammates and earn victories. But every once in a while, he was discouraged by the orphan-like discrimination he encountered.

Although not quite so athletic, I enjoyed tennis and played frequently with my friends. After investing in a few years of lessons, I began to play a consistently passable game and was eager to engage my children in the sport. I assumed that if they played I would be assured a partner with whom to hit balls. My daughters at that time did not have the patience to devote to learning the sport, but Ben did. Hitting tennis balls out of baskets after work and on weekend mornings became one of our favorite activities. As with anything involving balls, he was 100 percent engaged and quickly learned the sport.

By middle school Ben was enrolled in tennis clinics, and by high school, he was a solid player. Along the way he had to make some tough choices. He played soccer in all of the top flight leagues, basketball through the winter, and took an interest in hockey. We couldn't keep all of these sports going at full steam. It involved too much time and money for a single, working mom. So, much to my pleasure, especially since the practice hours were inhumane, hockey was dropped.

Our community focused more attention on the big stadium sports than on sports like tennis. Most of the youngsters whose parents could afford tennis lessons could also afford private school, so some of the talented tennis players left the public school system by the time high school rolled around. The social standing of a soccer or football star clearly outranked that of a tennis star in our high school. It should not have come as any great surprise to me when Ben balked at trying out for the tennis team. As a matter of fact, he completely tried to dodge the issue freshman year by hiding his racquet in his locker.

When I asked how the practices were going, Ben was evasive. Finally, we had a confrontation, and I pulled rank. The resultant deal was that he had to play at least one season to make good on the years out on the courts together and the lessons I had paid for. He finally agreed and begrudgingly showed up for practice.

Once on the court, Ben couldn't resist his innate drive to excel and earned himself a place on the varsity team playing doubles. He had a great season, and by his junior year he was the first singles player. His typical pattern was to hang back, watch his opponent's style, often losing a game or two in the process, and then go on the aggressive. This breath-holding strategy earned Ben the nickname "Net Ball," since the game's outcome always appeared to hang in the balance. Later, he used his tennis skills to earn money over the summer teaching in the recreation department and giving private lessons.

But the most fascinating part of this evolution has been the bigger lessons Ben learned, and how he has found numerous ways to transfer those lessons off the court and into his life. I have enjoyed watching this transference as much as I enjoyed sitting outside watching him play during the sports seasons. His stories about teaching youngsters the fun of the game, the focus required to play well, and most of all, the head game in tennis are delightful to hear. Those simple principles have helped Ben conquer many of his own challenges.

One instance occurred during tennis season in Ben's sophomore year in high school, while I was being treated for breast cancer. It was determined that I should have preventive surgery to reduce my risk of disease recurrence. The lengthy surgery was scheduled for a weekday during his season. Ben was playing second singles, and the team was counting on him for a win. That morning I asked him to play as usual rather than sit around in the OR waiting room all day. I knew that he would be climbing the walls, and I thought that a physical outlet would help distract him. Carelessly, I suggested that he bring home a win for me. Of course, Ben did just that. Later, when my head was on straighter, I realized the amount of pressure he must have felt. Fortunately he did win, and he uses this story as a motivator for his moodier players when he needs to make a strong point about leaving other problems off the court and completely focusing on the fun and skill in the game.

Ben's ability to move on after losing a point, change his strategy, and refocus on the next point was best demonstrated by his perseverance in getting admitted to medical school. Always a sharp math and science student, that part of the required MCAT testing was a breeze. But Ben's lack of reading speed and disinterest in books through his childhood came back to bite him on the verbal sections of the exam. Twice, he studied hard for the day-long test but could not quite figure out how to bring the verbal score up to par. Finally, he completely changed his strategy, bumped his score way up, and was accepted. I am not sure how many young people would be willing to take that awful exam three times, but Ben did and is on his way to becoming a physician.

The most important lesson Ben learned had to do with fairness. The years of overcoming other children's political advantages in school sports and having to get by on his own ability have stayed with him. I have never seen Ben give a child the advantage because of a parent's influence. I watch his eye for talent on and off the court and how he judges his peers and role models for their skills rather than their prestige. Ben's ability to see the good and the bad in an impartial way is a hard-earned gift from those years of proving his skills to others.

It is a constant inspiration to me and helps me look at others more objectively.

It is funny, though, that the best I can get from Ben these days is a mercy lesson on the court. Reminding him of the endless patience I had with him doesn't seem to earn me much slack. Ben always strives for the best and expects that from those around him, even me. I do enjoy, though, hearing about his future plans to be a coach for his children's sports teams and his determination to make sure that they find a sport they like to play. I just hope for their sakes that they are a little athletic.

Ben – 1st Singles high school

I Think I May Have Killed My Wig

I have never liked my wig, but I am too cheap to buy another one. I can't stand the idea of spending a lot of money on something that I absolutely hate. My wig was purchased ten years back when I lost most of my hair during breast cancer treatment. I almost donated it once and later tried to offer it to another cancer survivor undergoing treatment, but neither effort worked out. She, the wig, sat in my closet year after year, sometimes giving my husband or me a little jolt when we accidently stumbled upon it.

Since I really hate wearing it, I find her mostly good for laughs. Sometimes I leave her out on the Styrofoam frame just to scare people. Walking into our bathroom and seeing her backwards on the edge of the tub is sure to get a jump out of the poor victim. I even left her out in the bathroom last week knowing that the cleaning crew would have a start. Even though I wasn't there to enjoy the event, I smiled at work knowing that it would be happening any moment.

The best is when David puts it on. He has been bald since he was twenty, and I kind of think he enjoys wearing it. I must admit that it looks quite cute on him and has potential for some serious costume role-playing. If you squint a little, he looks like Herman, from the Hermits. Now, with no hair of my own, David thinks we look very extraterrestrial when we stand in the bathroom together getting ready for work. Who would have ever thought that he would have more hair than I?!

The first time I had cancer, I was very self-conscious about losing my hair and had a wig transition plan that I carefully implemented. The wig worked well during the day, and once home, I threw on a bandana.

My hair grew back quickly, so I went from a wig to quite short hair overnight. This time I am bald, irritated about losing my hair again, and find the wig itchy, distracting, and a general nuisance. I don't seem to care as much what others think about my efforts or lack to blend in. So, I wear scarves most of the time. The wig is saved for special occasions, typically times that it serves me best not to call unnecessary attention to myself, like when I have meetings at corporate headquarters, like this morning.

About a half hour before leaving for work, I put on the wig. Once on, I noticed that it smelled a bit dirty, so I decided to give her a shampoo. Thinking there was enough time, I bathed her and set her on the Styrofoam head to dry. She was a little stubborn and sat dripping as the time ticked on. So I pulled out my blow-dryer and attempted to speed things up. All seemed to be going pretty well until I noticed a few patches of crinkled up hair. The crinkling mounted by the second! My mind registered a big "uh oh," and I dunked her back in the water thinking that, like a bad curl, I could wash it out. Not so lucky—it looks like I may have murdered her after all. Now she reminds me of a white girl's "fro."

I wonder if I can get away with wearing her anyway. Perhaps I could try electric curlers; maybe those will help control the chaos I created. If not, I can try to blow through the next three months on scarves alone or face the music and spring for another wig. Knowing me, though, I may have a hard time resisting a crazy, red hooker wig. David suggested one of Tina Turner's looks.

Something about this hair loss seems to connect me with my cancer anger, and at the same time, it is bringing out the rebellious teenager that has lain dormant within me for the last thirty plus years. I freely admit that killing my wig gave me a strange sense of satisfaction, but I dare say I am not so sure that I am enjoying the consequences. Anybody out there with a spare wig?

Lessons from a Triathlete

As I reach the end of my second phase of treatment and prepare to head into the third and, God willing, last phase, I have found myself struggling with the mental preparation I need. For the most part, I have heard scary, uncomfortable details of what is ahead, and although this last part will only take three rounds of three treatments, each round seems like an enormous mountain to climb. Meanwhile, in the backdrop of my life are two, albeit unequal, life-altering events.

The first and by far most magnificent is that I am becoming a grandmother. Carrie's due date is right in the middle of my first week of intraperitoneal therapy (the chemo that is administered through my abdominal port), the worst part of the treatment regimen. Having delivered three children myself, I know that due dates are only educated guesses. Still, I am troubled by the possibility of having to watch through hazy, nauseous eyes rather than rooting for her every step of the way and having the physical reserve to hold her hand throughout the night if she needs it. A second event is that after three and a half months of frustrating setbacks, we are finally closing on our very own lake home. For David and me, this is a dream come true. I know that there will be pauses in my chemo when I should be able to enjoy it, but certainly not to the full extent that I would like. Oh well on that one.

The seeds of the triathlon concept began germinating a few weeks back when I was asked by a coworker what is ahead for me in treatment. I broke the process into three parts: surgery, intravenous chemotherapy, and intraperitoneal therapy. I sarcastically emphasized that the best part was saved for the finale, and I was currently nearing the end of part two. Each part has been tough with lots of unpleasant symptoms, but overall, I have been feeling up to returning to work and have been slogging through.

I began to mull over the triathlon analogy and started to think about its meaning more carefully. I reflected on some of the isolated nuggets of advice two of my close work friends, Liz and Gayle, have given me and began to see the patterns. Last week, Liz, a triathlete herself, shared insights about the mental game needed to take on the physical challenge of the events, and her words added more shape and form to the similarities. On a very simplistic level, it all boils down to a few easy strategies that I have put into a mental outline. My husband has accused me many times of thinking in bullets, and I suppose that I do. But what he doesn't realize is that bullets help me remember things. I am not quite as smart as he seems to think, especially with a good deal of "chemobrain" these days. Here are my survival bullets; ready, aim, fire:

- Stay positive, whatever it takes!
- Externally, keep the outsiders who bring me down far, far away. Stay away from worrisome conversations, people with sad faces, and what I call the "tsk, tsk" people at work and home. They only make it worse! I know that behind the behavior is mostly well meaning thoughts, but their discomfort in knowing the right thing to say or do is not my problem today. Once I heard a doctor refer to my case as "unfortunate." That word disturbed me so much that I was emotionally down all day.
- Internally, become the mother superior of my own self-discipline; no downer thoughts and no downer conversations. Look for the toe holds in the rock and keep pulling upward. Replace all of the negative baggage with rest and activities I enjoy, including work. Hell, why not! I am fighting cancer and deserve to have all of the satisfaction and fun I can rake in! This is the best time to be a caring friend to myself.
- Stay in the moment. When the moment is big, tiring, and at times physically overwhelming, don't add insult to injury by piling on more. As Liz might say, think about one stride at a time, and before you know it, you have

gotten a mile under your belt. I use some of the techniques learned in Lamaze and guided imagery to help get through the bad stuff. Breathing slowly and fully, thinking about peaceful places, and sometimes adding medications have helped take the edge off. Knowing, believing that the symptoms will pass—and they always do—has helped a lot. If I feel up to it, I get busy at work or at home to distract myself; and of course, I write.

- Remember the process. My therapy has been well studied, and great thought has gone into the risks and benefits connected with my treatment. So, like it or not, I have chosen to trust the science, medical therapy, physicians and nurses who are guiding me through the journey. Keep faith, trust, and hope alive.

Everyone around me seems to understand that I am in the middle of a physical triathlon of sorts, and 99 percent of the time, they give me a break if I step out of line. The positive thoughts I have received from my family and friends have helped keep my mental tank full, and as time goes on, those around me seem to sense when I need a lift or extra help. So, I pledge to remember that the next two and a half months will pass; I will take it one day at a time and make each day a positive addition to my life. In the end, I will finish this triathlon with a sense of accomplishment and pride. Today I plan to finish this essay, go for my treatment, and then assemble the baby's "home away from home" crib. I finally found all of the missing parts of my children's old crib in the attic.

To Sleep or Not to Sleep

Through most of my life, I have been one of those good sleepers. Trained from infancy to be very structured about bedtime, I have been consistent. My folks believed that lots of sleep strengthened the immune system, so we were the kids on the block in the summer in bed before sunset and up at the crack of dawn. In the early evening, Ann and I would lie in bed with the windows open to invite a cool breeze into our bedroom. We each had one stuffed animal that we named and played with in bed. Mine was a brown dog named Morgan (Moggie for short) that I would balance on my raised foot while I rested on my back waiting for fatigue to set in. Ann had a monkey she named Zippy.

We didn't care too much about being different because of our summer schedule until close to middle school. After that point, bedtime became a constant negotiation. Finally, Mom and Pop changed the rules in high school and allowed us to stay up until around 11:00 PM or midnight. It no longer mattered to them when we turned in as long as we slept ten hours; until college anyway, when ten hours was a pipe dream, literally.

Things stayed in that pattern for decades. I tried to keep sleep a priority, even through the child-bearing years, making sure that I had "power mom" naps to get me through the day. My children, except Ben, seemed to adapt to the plan quickly; so for the most part, we were a sleepy household at night.

This was until the cancer drugs came along. There are some amazing drugs on the market that fend off nausea and constipation, but wow, do they wreak havoc on the body rhythms. The steroids that are given through IV and orally are great at controlling chemo symptoms, but they also turn the sleep clock upside down and, I dare say, turn the wakeful hours on their side as well. The second time I took Ambien®, I woke up after eight restful hours (just like the commercial), got dressed for work, chatted with my husband, got into my car, and drove with double vision. Strangely, I thought by covering one eye, I could resolve the issue. Barely conscious, I drove bumping curbs and mailboxes on my way to work, sustaining $1,500 worth of damage to my right side of the car, including losing my side view mirror and slashing two tires en route! I could not recall anything that I said to anyone for a couple of more hours. I managed to call my daughter, Laura, who was on vacation, to chat with her about it, and she was so distressed that she called the oncologist. I have no recollection of making that phone call or damaging the car. Thanks to the tail effects of the drug, judgment and short-term memory were tossed out the window before I backed out of the driveway.

After pulling into a local garage that my mother and her friends used for the occasional ding they inflict on their cars, and where the proprietor was nicknamed Handsome Fred, I left my vehicle for a month of repairs. I called Laurie, one of my dear local friends, to help me get to work. First, I had agreed to hang at her house while the drugs wore off. By the time she got to the garage, I had forgotten that conversation and was cajoling her to take me to work for a day of meetings. She tried to get me to her house, but my power of temporarily cogent persuasion won out. I barely recall that as well. She wisely, and not too tactfully, suggested that I only listen and take copious notes at any meetings I had planned, since nothing coming out of my mouth at the time was making too much sense. I chose to follow her advice. She is a true girl friend, one who tells me if I have greens between my teeth. I did not doubt her for a moment.

But perhaps what I should have been listening to first were the numerous warnings issued during those TV commercials to which I barely pay attention. In my case, they were all true. As a matter of fact, I took an Ambien® last night, and for all I know, I may be writing this essay in a 5:00 AM fugue state!

Since that time, I try not to take any sleeping supplements the nights before I go to work. I can imagine how many hundreds of drivers out there are still working off the crazy effects of the drugs at sixty-five miles per hour on the highway, maybe even seeing double. But this drug-free plan leaves me open to some pretty strange wake-up times. I have developed a much more intimate relationship with the dark hours, and if I can't make myself get back to sleep, I usually get up and work or write, like now.

So, a warm and friendly 5:00 AM greeting to you early risers. A note of caution if you took something to sleep last night: go in late for work, get someone to quiz you on your short-term memory, and for heaven's sake, drive carefully!

Our New Lake Home

This morning David and I sat on our dock having a cup of coffee. As we looked out at the mist lifting off of the water and soaked in the early warmth of the day, we felt tremendous satisfaction with our new lake home. It has been over thirty years since my family sold our cottage on Swartswood Lake, and I have missed it ever since.

It seems like just yesterday that Ann, Leo, and I piled into our parents' car after school on Friday afternoons and headed for the lake. On the drive up, we passed corn fields, and Pop would belt out a few tunes from *Oklahoma*, only to elevate our moods further:

> Oh what a beautiful morning
> Oh what a beautiful day
> I've got a beautiful feeling
> Everything's going my way.
> —*Oklahoma*

After an hour we would pass Robbin's General Store and eagerly greet the first views of the lake with excitement and anticipation of the adventures that lay ahead.

Buying our lovely home was no easy task. It started about a year ago, when we realized that the cost and logistics of a family vacation for eight plus people had begun to feel like a difficult annual puzzle. Both David and I had grown up with summer homes, and the idea of finding one for our blended family seemed to be a perfect way to increase family time. We knew that it might mean visitors in bits and pieces rather than the entire crew on any given weekend, but we accepted that practical reality as part of the change a family grows through.

We spent months looking at every home listed within an hour's drive north of our house and became very familiar with the market. In the meantime, the economy was sinking and prices of homes were declining as well. This opened the door to houses otherwise over our heads, and after much searching, we found our home on Culver Lake. It took close to four months after we contracted to finally close. Problems with home appraisers and inspections held things up, and I developed cold feet after my diagnosis, but in the end, we bought the house. Again, David's unwavering optimism overtook my jittery nerves.

It boggles my mind that my memory skips back a full generation. Our children have completely missed the experience of growing up with a summer house. It will be our grandchildren whose sense of self will be influenced by the exploration of the water, woods, and beauty of nature that surrounds the area. Swimming, boating, and fishing will be as natural to them as it was to me. I see varying levels of connection as I watch our five children's reactions to this venture. Although there is plenty of excitement, imaginations are engaging at different rates. Mine seems to be racing ahead like a freight train.

I envision child-made aquariums, vaudeville shows on the dock, and grandchildren learning to swim and dive in the cool water. I see endless jigsaw puzzles, craft projects made with acorns and pieces of the outdoors, vegetable gardens, and maybe even sewing and knitting on rainy days. I imagine hosting our grandchildren on weekends when mom and dad need a little break and the special bond that will form with us because of this unique time alone. In my mind, I am happily toasting marshmallows and baking oatmeal cookies on chilly fall afternoons.

Oh, Baby!

Our little miracle! On September 9, shortly after 6:30 in the evening, Lily Taylor Hodge was born. Weighing in at six pounds and eleven ounces, she worked very, very hard squeezing her way down that universal passageway to life. Embraced in a family quilt of support, mommy, daddy, and infant were wrapped in so much love that the room was pulsating. The hospital bent a few rules so that Carrie could have numerous coaches to support her through the birth. Many pictures were taken, even more tears were shed, but the overwhelming feeling of instantaneous love for this new life was felt by everyone present.

Lily was a small package. We all thought that she was going to be a big baby. Instead, she was tiny, with a perfect face, a full head of blondish hair, and flawless skin. At the incubator, her aunt Laura and I exchanged glances and shared the surprise of a six-pounder rather than an eight-pound baby. She was a cuddle bun from the start, a little slow to pink up and initially lazy at mommy's breast. But with the nursing support and her mom and dad's silent patience, she caught on and is getting with the program now.

Lily's bassinet was kept in the hospital room most of the time, and that made it nice for visitors to meet her. Birth is a bit overwhelming, both physically and emotionally, so the crowds of family and friends needed to be the right size. That was accomplished with little effort on everyone's parts. After two full days, Lily came home to her beautiful house and to a very gorgeously personalized baby room. This little girl has it all; lots of love, dreams, devoted parents, family, and friends, but most of all, a sense of belief from those around her that as she grows she can take on her goals, live her life in a fulfilling way, and feel the happiness that each day brings. Knowing my daughter, Carrie, and her husband, Erin, as I do, they will make her earn these accomplishments, confident that nothing of real value comes cheaply. But this will be done in a loving way so that Lily's life is one of strength and not self-doubt.

Ironically, what no one but my sister seemed to recall, was that exactly six years earlier, Lily's great-grandpa, Robert (Pop), passed away in the same hospital. The date had a strange déjà vu feeling to me, but I was so wrapped in the moment of the delivery and birth that I did not make the connection. Later when reminded, I was emotionally moved by this perfect circle of life; one treasured existence gaining closure while a new one enters to fill the space left behind.

I must say though, little Lily, Great-Grandpa wore size eleven shoes, mighty big ones to fill, especially with your tiny feet. I suspect, though, that you will make a footprint of your own having your unique signature, just as Great-Grandpa Robert did. We will all love every single minute watching that happen! Welcome to the world, our precious new treasure.

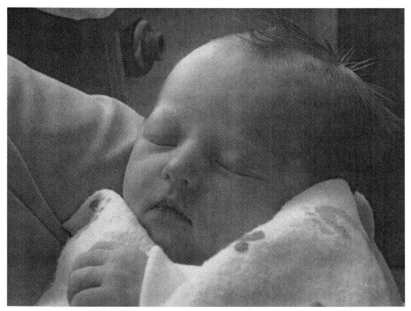

Lily, 1 day old

Who's Been Eating the Nuts Off of the Coffee Cake? My Yom Kippur Confession

Me ... me ... me ... yes, for all of you doubters, it has been me all of these years. I can't stop myself. I have no defenses around the impulse. From the time I was a little girl and saw my mother sneaking those nuts off ... well, suffice to say, I was helplessly out of control!

I know I have ruined many bakery breakfast treats with this behavior and am a little ashamed that for years I lied about it. Eventually, I had to give up the treat all together to control the impulse. But this addiction was, and still is, well established, and I make no attempt to control it anymore. I do a bit better with pecan pie, only leaving behind the crusts. As far as baklava is concerned, I eat every last morsel. But give me a dessert with those sweet nuts, and they are all my eyes can see.

Since I am into confessions, I will also admit to something else. There have been a couple times, no, a few times, that I have kept too much change at a store, justifying that a sloppy sales clerk is due some consequences. The last time I did this, probably over a decade back, I felt guilty for so long that I swore off it. Now the consequence is dealing with me while I ask her/him to recheck my change. Somehow, I get the feeling that most clerks would prefer things the old way.

I'm really lousy at white lies, and I'm not sure why. During my adolescence I was concerned that I had become a pathological liar. My poor folks had to suffer through a few years of that behavior while my nut of choice was the high school bad boy from the other side of the tracks. Our mutual realization that the relationship was kaput was the only reason it finally ended. After that, I did a complete one-eighty,

113

relieved to finally be able to tell the truth. I practiced honesty so much and did it so well that I forgot to study the looks on peoples' faces while I shared my views with them. Hurt feelings, embarrassment, anger, and what may have been interpreted as oppositional behavior ruled the day.

I figured that to be in my inner circle, one had to be tough enough to take me on. Fortunately, this did not last terribly long. My rapidly shrinking inner circle of friends became equally honest with me, and I got a dose of my own medicine. So, I learned to ease up a bit and use more tact, and I discovered what I have come to refer to as the political highroad.

The political highroad is often not so interesting. It's certainly not the stuff that makes great stories or TV content, but it does seem to work most of the time. I'm sure there are instances when others sense I am trying to be diplomatic and think I am insincere. Somehow I must be giving off other honesty cues that are tipping them off. My children accused me for years of yelling at them when I hadn't even opened my mouth. They always seemed to know when I was displeased. There have been a few coworkers who have responded in a similar way when I haven't even done anything—yet—but I think at this point of my life it may be the best I can do.

So, yes, it was me who ate those nuts. Consider yourselves forewarned. If you dare buy a coffee cake ring and leave me alone with it, don't be surprised if five minutes later it looks pockmarked and no longer presentable. To that I say, "Can't say I didn't warn you!"

Free Fall: The Final Frontier

In my one-day-at-a-time mindset, I have chosen to face each chapter of my cancer journey in bite-sized steps. Now, as I finish up my final intraperitoneal treatments, I need to brace myself to face the final frontier. This phase is radically different and will last the rest of my life. It consists of rigorous, three-month follow-up testing, including blood work and sometimes CT scans. My best recollection from the breast cancer years is that this cycle of so-called life renewal is better described as sheer panic every three months immediately before and following the testing. I suppose it is now time to figure out my next coping strategy. Do I dare allow myself to feel normal again while living with so much uncertainty? Denial after the breast cancer was a pretty effective strategy the last ten years. I know that this time the solution will require a blend of the controlled fight for survival, my focus for the last six months, with some degree of peacefully accepting the surrender that goes with this next leg of the journey. So far, distractions seem to work well for me, along with my trusty mantra, "Don't look down."

My first objective and distraction is to get myself back into fighting form. I have at least ten steroid-added pounds to lose, stamina to rebuild, hair to grow back, and I must phase back into a full day at work. I have a thirty-guest Thanksgiving celebration planned at my home and our traditional *Chranukka* celebration in late December, complete with gift buying for eleven family members plus work friends. For those unfamiliar with this blended religious tradition, we take what we have identified as the best qualities of Hanukkah and Christmas (we have spouses and boyfriends/girlfriends covering the whole spectrum) and blend those traditions into one wonderful night of celebration.

Generally it consists of lighting a Menorah, eating brisket, latkes and applesauce, having delectable Christmas deserts, and then opening our presents, all of them at one seating. My children have also encouraged me to have an end-of-chemo *La'Chaim* (To Life) party in December with appetizers and dessert. That will be a wonderful way to thank all of my angels and distract me until the New Year.

After New Years, I have committed to present a topic at a national symposium in Phoenix, followed by a mom/daughter spa getaway in Scottsdale, a long overdue thank you to my wonderful daughters who helped me through the surgery and treatments. My oldest even had a delicious little baby to help me through it! Timing is truly everything. My husband and I are planning a trip to Hawaii in March, a state we have both been eager to visit. In between it all will be a concentrated refocus on work. We have ambitious plans this year and much work to do. But between these great events will be two or three rounds of testing. Maybe that is what Ativan® and lots of deep breathing is for. I really haven't figured out this part yet. I hate it when the waiting anxiety returns.

I know that this cancer experience has changed me in many ways. My journal captures much of it. The reflections have served as self-therapy, reminding me how full my life story has been. I somehow wonder, though, whether the changes in my outlook are noticeable. Will others see me as too soft, a sign of weakness in my work place? I wonder if I can hold onto the balance of strength and add to that my growing sensitivities and insights about life and others. Will the cancer experience make me feel stronger or more fragile? Who will understand? Maybe they will all figure that the drugs made me a bit crazier.

Looking back a decade, one important change that took place after my bout with breast cancer was that I worked very hard to influence other decision makers at work to go the extra mile to keep patients in the center of the care model. I had the opportunity, after my final breast surgery, to lead the Women's Center development project, and the first step came with commitments from the medical staff to adhere to a performance model where the reading of mammograms and other films was completed in twenty-four hours. Our nurse navigator had a hotline for patients anxious to get their results. We layered in newer models for biopsies and added a complementary medicine department right next door, complete with a private room equipped with a massage chair for patients who were waiting for procedures. All of these decisions began with an eye on the patients' needs.

In the last decade, I have kept this focus but now feel it more strongly. I hope that in my organization, my recent cancer experience will help others understand why I push so hard to keep our patients the primary focus. In the end, with so many "customers" in medicine, it is easy to set the patient off to the side. The irony is that without that crucial focus, we will never have a real bull's-eye in our effort to be the best hospital system in our region.

So, I have many meaningful distractions to keep my mind off of my plight and my fight for survival. I have effective mantras and some medications to lean on if needed. Most of all, I have my extraordinary family and the stories of love and adventure that have defined us.

During my treatment and recovery these last six months, I have watched and read more news than ever before. I am shocked and disheartened by the daily reports of the loss of life in the Middle East and Africa and sometimes here at home. These lives are lost in a second without regard to human value. The victims are given no warning or opportunity to protect themselves. Here at home, drivers speed recklessly on our highways in some type of artificially induced rage or while intoxicated, putting many lives at risk. And we know now that the Ambien® commercials aren't kidding around about sleepwalking, or in my case sleep-driving. That morning commute has to be pretty dicey for lots of our neighboring cars on the road. It all leads me to think about how life can, and often, leave us so suddenly without early warning signs, preventive measures, or a chance to fight.

In my case, I have been given the opportunity to fight hard for my life, and I plan to continue watching for any early warning signs of danger ahead. Who knows, with more cancer breakthroughs on the horizon, I may be participating in a new model of care down the road. After all, as a good friend of mine once said, "In a cosmic sense, we all spend much more time dead than alive. It is best to work hard to keep those living years going as long as possible."

Role Reversals

A month after my final chemotherapy treatment, my now twenty-four-year-old son Ben called me at eight o'clock in the evening to discuss recliners. At the time, I was on my second martini in a Fort Lauderdale restaurant and having quite a good time. Typically a one-drink kind of gal, I was cutting loose and enjoying the delicious food and company of my two stepsons and husband in a funky little downtown restaurant. I had gone six months with traumatized taste buds that were, for all practical purposes, dead to the world. Now that chemo was over, food and liquor never tasted so divine.

This brings me to my point. My son, who is quite accustomed to having me on high alert day or night to discuss any topic of his choosing, was not prepared to discover Mom in an inebriated state. My silliness caught him by surprise. He was clearly caught off guard hearing me behave with a lack of adult restraint.

Bear in mind that Ben's startled reaction came from the very same young man who as a high school student routinely held parties in our basement whether I was home or not. The typical drill back then involved me waking up around 2:00 AM to the sound of beer pong-related laughter, and moments later, Ben dashing up the steps exclaiming, "It's okay, Mom. We're cool, we're cool. I have everything under control." A few years afterward, this debauchery advanced to pledging a fraternity, adopting new brothers (who the heck were these new family members anyway?), and even living in a frat house with a disconnected toilet sitting in the hall of the second floor. My only thought at the time was hepatitis.

But this reaction also came from that very same person who sat with me during all-day intraperitoneal infusion treatments and watched my abdomen fill up with pounds of poisonous fluid. Just last month when I needed to have that port surgically removed (it had served its purpose and was getting infected), Ben took me to the OR, kept me company before and after the procedure, and then stayed with me at home while the effects of the anesthesia wore off.

It has been over two months since my treatment ended, and I incorrectly assumed that my children had permitted themselves to slip back into normal lives and shake off their concerns about my health. Did cancer make them get old before their time? Did my being sick make this happen, or is it typical for them to be happy settling down and entering a tamer, more grownup life? Will this role reversal be permanent? I sure don't remember the turntable of time moving so far and so fast. And since when does a twenty-four-year-old care about Barcaloungers on a Saturday night?! I am still getting over the parental trauma of raising teenagers, and they have moved on to worrying about me and recliners. What happened to midlife? Is this yet another curse that comes with cancer? What is the big hurry?

I am just beginning to acclimate to the gradual role reversal with my own mother. But, the more I sense my kids' concern and a potential intrusion in my life, the more I empathize with her. I find myself giving the high sign to my eighty-four-year-old mother and saying, "Do whatever you want, Mom. Go have some fun, and if someday you want to be carried out of the house feet first instead of living in an adult community, that is also fine with me." I fully understand her need for independence and have few to no guilt-driven restrictions. After all of her years devoted to my loving but in-command father, she deserves to call as many shots as she can.

So far, my only request is that Mom restrict her traveling to countries that are within an eight-hour plane ride of Newark Airport. Fortunately, she has gotten Asia and South Africa out of her system. Somehow the thought of going that far away to bring her home is a bit difficult for me to wrap my head around. It would take the entire plane ride there to shake off my irritation. Luckily, she has been very healthy and energetic. Mom's biggest problem is keeping her travel friend's enthusiasm for future trips as high as hers. I suppose there might come a day for both of us when we must look down a generation for assistance and guidance, but given our current level of function, that isn't likely to happen any time too soon.

What no one warned me about was that the next stage in this cancer experience is getting everyone to chill out and relax; give me my personal space back and get normal again. Yeah, I don't know for sure how long it will last, but it beats standing in alert waiting for the next shoe to drop. And if I can be nimble enough to dodge imaginary shoes falling from the sky then that dance will need to be the next one I teach to my children.

Soft Breathing

I lay in bed listening to the sounds of soft breathing. On my right is Carrie, fast asleep and making quiet noises that sound like a soft desert breeze. She is resting, feeling very much at peace in her comfortable bed at the spa in Scottsdale. Yesterday, she had waves of tears as she thought about her little baby at home. Although Lily was under the careful watch of her dad and sitter, Carrie had never left her for such a long time, and the baby was pulling at her heart strings.

Yesterday, during an afternoon shopping excursion in Old Scottsdale, we walked into a women's lounge in Nordstrom only to stumble on "baby central." There were three moms sitting expressionless on couches nursing their infants, looking too much like cows in a dairy barn. Another new mother was changing her seven-week-old's diapers. Her baby was furious and filling the air with screams. The scene came down like a fist on Carrie's very sensitive heart and her eyes quickly filled with tears. In contrast, Laura and I simply couldn't stop laughing. The entire scene seemed like a cruel but amazingly well-orchestrated joke.

Carrie was a dream baby. She was calm and peaceful and slept through the night when she was only four weeks old. Like a little doll, I could pick her up from her crib to show her off to friends and then lay her down to return to sleep. She initiated me into motherhood and awakened new emotions and responsibilities. She taught me how it felt to fall deeply in love with your child, a force of nature that one has to experience to fully understand. It was so compelling, that if I were not stopped, I could have filled my house with ten children. Later, Laura and Ben evoked that same tug, one far beyond any voluntary control.

Although a grandmother now, I rejoice in the force of emotion growing between Lily and me; what a wonderful, loving feeling.

Laura is sharing a bed with me. She alternates between silent breathing and what sounds like whispers coming from her soft lips. I flash back over twenty-five years and recall the nightly routine of tiptoeing into their bedroom to make triple certain that they were comfortably sleeping. I used to pause at the doorway and soak in the wonders of my two little girls softly breathing in their beds. They shared a room during those first few years; Carrie in her big-girl bed and Laura in the crib. While Carrie had crib toys to play with as a baby, Laura had chosen Carrie. Aside from her blanket that she loved for far too many years, her idea of stimulation was watching her sister Carrie. I used to laugh walking into the room seeing her blue saucer-shaped eyes peering over the bumper pads watching her big sister. She didn't want to miss a thing Carrie was doing. A couple of years later, when she graduated into her twin bed, Laura would sneak out, landing on the floor with a thud, and scurry over to Carrie's bed to play. Hearing the patter of her little feet, I would call out, "Laura, are you in your bed?" She would answer back, "Yes, Mommy," while she scampered back to her own bed, giggling all the way.

Carrie and Laura are sisters and will always have that complex connection. Now in their early adult years, they are once again tightly bonded as they support each other, laugh at their inside jokes, and compare notes on more adult topics. They have found love, felt hurt, and matured into professionals in their fields. Oh, they still bicker as well, and I frequently find myself asking them to tone it down. That will probably never change.

My daughters have been there for me and for each other. There is simply no other way to put it. They have both been able to manage their fears about my health and focus on helping me through the challenges of surgery and treatment. They are extraordinary young women, and this spa vacation was my way of recognizing their support. The venue seemed perfect for all of our recoveries. It has given us time to rest, reminisce, and talk about future dreams.

Yesterday, we hiked Camelback Mountain near the resort. From a distance it seemed pretty innocent, and I remembered having hiked it before almost twenty years ago while on a tennis girl's getaway. Carrie and Laura thought it would be a good challenge and rewarding accomplishment for us to share together. I had second, third, and fourth thoughts about an eighth of a mile into the trail. It was full of steep inclines, guard rails, and large boulders to scramble. It took over two hours to climb the one-mile, uphill, rock climbing trail. The only reasons I didn't turn around were my girls' coaching, their determination to help me up the mountain—"Mom, just take one rock at a time"—and the harder reality that returning down that very trail looked more dangerous and exhausting than continuing up. Finally at the summit, we enjoyed the views, had a snack, and headed down a different trail to the base. This one was terrifying at the top, no protection preventing hikers from falling down either side of the sharp peak. I managed to weave my way down, mostly sliding on my butt, feeling very grateful for a low center of gravity. None of it seemed to faze the girls as they bounced down the rocks like a couple of monkeys.

Yes, this morning I again laid in bed listening to their breathing. No longer did it sound so innocent. The slightest movement of my limbs sent waves of muscle pain everywhere. Stillness was my only defense, so I lay motionless listening. Did this extreme activity help me bond? I think not. Certainly the last six months was enough extreme activity for me. But it showed me what my daughters are capable of. I am proud that they are comfortable taking on hard challenges. Their grit to keep moving forward reassures me that the next female generation of my family is rock solid.

Scottsdale, AZ, 2010

Newton's Third Law

Once I finished with the chemotherapy, I decided to live out my dreams to the best of my physical and financial potential. This decision to live life to the fullest brought my husband and I to Hawaii for two weeks. In my determination to squeeze in every last ounce of fun, this was the second vacation I dropped quickly into the calendar. I figured that being in the United States (we are reminded in all tour books that the Hawaiians are very sensitive to this fact), I could play travel agent on my own. So far that has made for a very interesting trip.

David, my partner in paradise, and I cashed in close to a hundred thousand airline points that had accumulated over the last few years and booked first-class seats for the ten-and-a-half-hour flights to and from Honolulu. I had never been on such a long flight, and first class turned out to be a very good move. Even after all of the cancer-related emotions, it is strange that I continue to be a jittery passenger on flights. One might think that, by now, I'd have nerves of steel. I've never really been sure why I get nervous, perhaps it is the lack-of-control feeling, the realization that a crash is generally fatal, the fear of free fall through the air, or the remote possibility that there is some whack job on the plane with explosives in his crotch. Who knows, but strangely, I was totally relaxed this time around while we flew at 550 miles per hour covering close to 6,000 miles and five hours of time change.

Knowing that there were lots of good hotel deals in these post-recession days, and also wanting to stay at some of the swankier resorts, I hunted around for bargains. In Maui, I found a great deal at one of the better hotels: five nights with one night free. In an effort to provide high-end customer service, these places now have their customer relations reps reaching out to you by e-mail weeks ahead of your trip to see when you plan on arriving, likes and dislikes, any services that you would prefer planned in advance, and the clincher question: is this some type of special occasion?

After starting out ten months back whispering the word cancer and not wanting anyone badgering me with questions, I have now done an about-face and am much freer with my banter about the past year, even writing a memoir for all to see. I let this lovely woman know that our trip wasn't a honeymoon, anniversary (we are just approaching nine years), or big birthday, but the end of six months of cancer treatment, and in some form, a celebration of life and good health. I told her that I would be easy to spot, the tall woman with very short hair. Well, that seemed to resonate with her. After all, who hasn't known someone stricken with this disease?

After a few days on the island, I could see that Maui is for wealthy Californians what Boca is for their New York counterparts, with over-bronzed older men trying to reclaim their youth and very blonde, long-ago California beauties. There is an abundance of this younger geriatric set milling about the golf courses, sipping martinis in expensive restaurants and talking about how much longer before their kids bring the grandchildren for a visit. Cancer and cardiac talk is everywhere.

My husband, who has totally enjoyed the cancer perks along this journey, was delighted to learn that this woman, on hearing of the reason for our trip, secretly upgraded us to an ocean view king suite, complete with a fully appointed kitchen, dining room, and triple-sized balcony. For a couple of weary travelers, this was quite a nice surprise. As a matter of fact, he immediately checked with me to see if I had alerted the other hotels about our "occasion." I thought that I had.

The next day, at the concierge desk while booking some dinner reservations, I asked the attendant to pass along our thanks to the reservations department for the upgrade. After planning the events of the next couple of days, we took off for whale watching, and then headed out for dinner at a local restaurant. Our waitress, a middle-aged woman with what my father would describe as a stage whisper, took our order and then, in a booming voice that could be heard throughout the establishment (and maybe as far away as The Big Island), congratulated me on finishing chemotherapy. I practically choked on my sparkling water while managing to ask her, "How could you possibly know that?"

She replied that the concierge filled her in, and that she was a thirty-six-year survivor herself.

David, who is a very private person, wasn't pleased. Health-care privacy violations ran through our minds as every head in the place seemed to turn toward us, and some sadly nodded in understanding. Gulping down my embarrassment, I thanked her and turned my attention back to my husband, who was still looking a bit stunned. I managed to laugh, seeing the poetic justice that came with milking things the way I had. After all, as Newton proved a very long time ago, "For every action, there is an equal and opposite reaction." Lesson to self: be careful playing the cancer card.

The Third Act

During the year following my separation, close to twenty years ago, I dated a compassionate man also going through a divorce. Both of us were pretty wounded from our experiences and, more than anything else, needed empathetic friends. For the better part of a year, that was all we were for each other—understanding shoulders. Once the healing began to set in, it became clear that we were not particularly well suited, so we parted amicably, going our separate ways. But one great thing I remember about him was his love for planning activities, and after the previous few years on my emotional roller coaster, I was totally game.

On one of those outings, we saw the play *Our Town,* by Thornton Wilder. The story centered on an ordinary set of characters in a New England town and sent its universal message of love, companionship, and disappearing into life's rhythms through the simplicity of its characters and staging. I was completely drawn in and found the play enjoyable until the third act, when Emily, who died in childbirth, barters for just one more day among the living.

In this final act, Emily, against the advice of others buried beside her in the town cemetery, is transported to her parent's kitchen on her twelfth birthday. Her mother and father move through their morning routine simply going through the motions, never really experiencing anything fully. Emily struggles to capture their attention, but they don't sense her need to connect. She is left feeling lonely, isolated, and disappointed, realizing the simple truth: one should embrace every moment in life while it lasts.

I sat in my seat and quietly wept, thinking about the sense of loss around my marriage and how it was absorbing practically all of my energy. I thought about my very young children and how emotionally unavailable I had become to them. And I thought about all of the dreams I had for my family and for me that I had all but relinquished. I was only thirty-three years old and had allowed myself to believe the world had slipped out of the palm of my hand. I had lost my grip.

I realized my life had to change, and only I could make that happen. The epiphany that life is a gift hit me hard that day, twelve years before my first cancer diagnosis and seven years before my younger brother, Leo, passed away. The fact that, as Emily discovered, life can be taken unexpectedly struck home with me. She learned her lesson too late to impact herself or others. I did not want to experience those regrets.

Looking back now, I know that day was a turning point. For my friend, sitting next to me weeping must have felt like the date from hell. But after that play, I slowly began to follow a new imperative. Oh, there were plenty of slipups; just ask my friends and kids, they know the truth. But Emily's misfortune gave me a meaningful reminder to value all of the moments we are given in life, and when I feel overwhelmed, I often think about Emily and the lessons she learned too late.

A few years ago, I noticed a poster in the hospital where I worked. It was a close-up photo of a nurse holding the hand of a very sick patient. The caption read something like, "The closer we come to death, the tighter we hold onto life." It seems to be a universal truth that we all want to keep living, no matter how old and frail we become. But to live without feeling value every day is a very sad thing. I think that the greatest loss of all is to come to the end, only to realize all of the moments taken for granted.

So, as I take a deep breath and continue on with my life, I look forward to many wonderful times ahead, some shared and some that I enjoy alone. My personal and family stories will continue to define and shape my future. I have given myself permission to let go of the fears that surround living with cancer, inventorying them and then putting them all in a box, like the rabbi suggested nine months ago when I saw him in his study. Just as I have found the courage to face the hard times up to this point, I choose to believe that I have the confidence and grit to face whatever lies ahead. I have found that it is much simpler to tune into the moment and enjoy the riches around me than spend my time handwringing, worrying about all of the ifs. When I stop and experience the moment I am in, my senses begin to sharpen. I feel the hint of spring in the air, I notice the beauty of the world around me, and I feel the deep warmth in the embraces of my family and friends.

About the Author

A lifelong resident of New Jersey, Jane Rubin has spent over twenty-five years as a healthcare administrator in hospital systems throughout the state. She earned her undergraduate degree and a master's degree in speech pathology from the University of Michigan, an MBA from Washington University, and presently serves as Director of Neuroscience for Atlantic Health System. Jane lives in Randolph, New Jersey, with her husband, David, an attorney.

"*Almost a Princess* eloquently captures the emotional journey of a cancer survivor. Author and survivor Jane Rubin courageously opens her heart as she takes us beyond the disease and helps us feel hope, strength, peace and healing."

Trisha Meili, Best Selling Author, *I Am The Central Park Jogger: A Story of Hope and Possibility*

"Jane Rubin has written a memoir that is wonderfully inspiring and full of insights about her cancer experience within the context of a very full and meaningful life. *Almost a Princess* invites the reader to experience the courage, humor, and coping strategies of a woman determined to drink from a glass half full."

David M. Gershenson, MD
Chairman, Foundation for Women's Cancer
J. Taylor Wharton, M.D. Distinguished
Chair in Gynecologic Oncology
Department of Gynecologic Oncology and
Reproductive Medicine, Unit 1362
University of Texas M.D. Anderson Cancer Center

"The powerful essays in *Almost a Princess* describe the hope and courage of a survivor of two deadly diseases. Cancer patients, their families and their friends will read Jane's stories and appreciate the importance of coping and thriving through these horrible diseases. As a clinician/ investigator, I am humbled by the bravery that our patients display."

Brian M. Slomovitz, MD, MS, Director of Research,
Carol G. Simon Cancer Center
Associate Director, Women's Cancer Center, Atlantic Health, N.J.

The Mathilda Fund

Half of the royalties of *Almost a Princess* will be donated to the Mathilda Fund, a designated account for ovarian cancer research. By purchasing this memoir, you have provided vital support for this important cause.

Who was Mathilda? When I began writing this book, what I had in mind was a self-healing journal. Over time, I became more comfortable with the writing process and felt a greater need to write for future generations of my family and also other cancer survivors who might relate to my experiences. As the project continued to mature, I envisioned an additional purpose, research funding.

As of publication time, I am a subject in a clinical trial designed to reduce recurrence of ovarian cancer. As an ovarian/peritoneal cancer patient, I have become all too familiar with the limited menu of clinical trials. Although great strides have been made in the past few years, there are still volumes to learn.

I began by tracing my BRCA 1 defect back in time as far as I could. I knew that it had been passed down through the paternal side of my family, but none of my first cousins or my mother could recall my great grandmother's name. She died before my father was born in 1923 so Pop never knew her. Her only child, Julian, my grandfather, passed away in 1975. According to family folklore, she died of a "woman's disease." I had also heard, growing up, that Julian was the surviving infant of twins. The other child was a girl but no one knew her name, so I began hunting online to find out more.

What I discovered was that she was born in Germany in February 1865 and immigrated to the United States in 1866, after the Civil

War ended. She and her much-older husband, Abraham, whom she reportedly married at 16, appeared in a 1900 New York City census report. They and Julian, then 18, were recorded living in a tenement house in the Lower East Side along with other Jewish families and two Irish couples. There were few other facts I could find on my own. I had hit a dead end and found myself lying in bed at night imagining the rest of her life story.

I don't think I will ever know all of the facts, but she most likely developed symptoms of ovarian/breast cancer in her late 30s or 40s, sometime after that census report. At the turn of the 20th century, cancer was still viewed as a socially taboo disease, and she probably hid her symptoms as long as possible. Medically speaking, little could be done at that time. I imagine she eventually died a painful, lonely death. Adding insult to injury, just two generations later, no one could even remember her name.

It was Mathilda.

CPSIA information can be obtained at www.ICGtesting.com

260528BV00001B/45/P